THE CONFLENT TALES

Volume 2

LYVYNG YN PARADYSE

STORIES FROM A PYRENNEAN PARADISE THROUGH THE VOICES OF THOSE WHO LIVE THERE

Contents of Volume 2

Prologue

The Prologue to the Conflent Tales

Purists may wonder why this prologue is included in both the Conflent Tales Books. That's partly because someone, somewhere, without the essential knowledge that there are in fact two volumes of tales needs to be reminded of the sheer rhetorical and literary beauty of this introduction. And partly to annoy readers who ask the question in the first place. Whatever, here it is in its full pristine fabulous wonder.

The drofte of Merche's root has been truly perced and April is dripping with soote shoures. Another journey has begun. Those of you who haven't sampled the delights of Chaucer's Prologue to the Canterbury Tales whilst dozing in the back row of a hot schoolroom may be wondering whether you have picked the right language. In that case start here! That was just a bit of show. There again, those of you who have read volume 1 will be experiencing that feeling of déjà vu and wondering why we're repeating the prologue here. Well that's because not everyone reads books in chronological order. Some crazy people, and you may be one of them, seem to do things backwards and read volume 2 before volume 1. And anyway it's a fun piece.

So here beginneth a new and different prologue. For Canterbury read Conflent – that's not a bad swap. For Chaucer read Longworth – well, you can't have it all! Hold on a tick. The Conflent – where's that? Nowhere near Canterbury, that's for sure. It's about a 1000 miles further South and in a different country. So will this travel book last 700 years like the first one? Who knows, but the odds are that it will be as durable as the thousand year Reich was. There's one thing in its favour – it isn't your standard travel guide. They're so dull. Go here, go there, see this, see that, stay in this hotel, avoid that restaurant. Nothing about what makes a region tick. Nothing about the people, except occasionally the historical toffs who were born there, and they're usually dead. Nothing to give the reader insights into the manners, mores, habits, lives, loves, pain and laughter that gives the true story of a real place where real people live. Nothing to unlock the door to the secret garden of a region and lay bare its true soul. Until now! And so, it is with such an excruciating mixed metaphor that we unfold the Conflent Tales.

In effect, this is a travel book, a set of adventure stories and a confessional all rolled into one, and brought to the reader through the mouths of those who live in this hidden paradise. And it's funny. Gosh it's funny. Subtly, rhetorically and guffawly funny. If there were a muse for laughter, which of course there isn't since the Greek muses didn't have much of a sense of humour and didn't think to train one up, she would have heartily approved of this book.

When the opening caste of the book first purchased their Conflent farmhouse in 1989, they were not expecting to make it a permanent residence. At that time they were returning to England from a six year stretch in Paris and Brussels, and both work obligations and the other commitments of two busy lives seemed to stretch a long way into the future. Professing and Nursing were the thieves of all their time. The opportunity to think about anything more than a week ahead was a rare luxury. But fortune's finger and idle circumstance around 1992 combined to make such a move a possibility, and after a long and introspective reflection, that possibility was transformed into fact a year later. The journey into the paradise of the Conflent had begun. From being a place to visit 2 or 3 times a year to become immersed in paint tins, garden cuttings and mortar, the *mas* des Oliviers became the centre of the universe - a huge 3-storey dog kennel for Artur into which he gladly invited us, if only to open the tins of pedigree pal. And a reason to write these tales of the heart of a region through its actors.

It is said, with some trepidation by those who would rather keep the secret, that the Conflent will be the next region of France to attract the foreign invader, the Dordogne, Riviera and Provence having become too expensive. The *franc fort*, which made the pound look like monopoly money in the mid-nineties, was first superceded by the *livre fort*, in which Brits in their thousands searched for a place to call their own in foreign fields. More recently the *euro fort*, after fluctuating like a Greek tax break, joined the eurozone slide into oblivion, and the pound/euro exchange rate once more favoured the brits. Only to be undone more rcently by the mass delusions of grandeur caused by the black Brexit plague. Only the most prescient of soothsayers can predict what will happen in the future, but the new situation hasn't reanimated the invasion of l'*Albion perfide'* to these elysian pastures. The credit crunch and its aftermath didn't help of course. House prices slid downwards in inverse ratio to bankers' bonuses. It's still in a deep depression that neither whisky nor hypnotherapy can halt. But it will return. The Conflent has all the advantages of climate, mountain environment, relative cheapness of property and a people desperate to experience the wonders of cricket. It is as far as one can get from England and still be in France, with the splendours of Spain close by. Where else can one pluck a luscious ripe peach while looking out at a 9000 foot snow-capped mountain, typing a book out on a sunny balcony surrounded by rolling hills and verdant valleys, with a babbling brook flowing by and the nightingales just tuning up for their evening symphony - as I am doing at the present moment. If there is a mosquito within two miles, the local entomological society will want to know about it.

But all paradises also have a dark side. Despite, perhaps because of, its great beauty, the Conflent is a region of high unemployment and barely hidden poverty. So these tales have another purpose and that is to bring in greater wealth from tourism. Anyone who reads them and doesn't want, nay yearn, to visit the Conflent might consider donating their heart for use at the Eus boulodrome. Hidden in the midst of the light-heartedness and laughter there is a more important message. Readers who get as far as chapter ten receive not only the biscuit but an insight into why it was written. And yet, in the last twenty years our intrepid travellers have met so many wonderful people, heard so many marvellous stories and survived so many blissful experiences that our heroes couldn't keep the secret any longer. They had to tell it and so did their animals and the people for whom the Conflent is ingrained in their bones. Others might hate them for blowing the gaff, but here, in the Conflent, is the journey into paradise, related through the lives of the people who found and founded it.

Norman Longworth
Eus, France

Norman Longworth is a former professor who has published many fascinating/boring academic books and papers that sell to other fascinating/boring academics around the world. He has a world-wide reputation for setting up lifelong learning cities and you can't get more fascinating/boring than that. However in his self-published books there is another Norman Longworth – one set free from the chains of academia and who sees publishing as a playground for using words creatively and telling stories. His books so far are travel books with a difference but he intends to branch out with a wide variety of poetry forms, including the doggerel verse of 'lancashire monologues' - an artform that flourished in his native region in the late 19h and early 20th centuries. When not professing or writing he golfs badly, plays the piano excruciatingly and sings melodiously in his South of France home. He can be contacted through his website www.longlearn.org.uk

Dedication

This book is dedicated to the hundreds of interesting and friendly people we have met in this most beautiful region of France. It is also dedicated to those not so friendly ones who thankfully are in a very small minority. My wife and I, royal inference not intentional, have been accepted by the vast majority of the Catalans, and the *Catalans adoptés* from other parts of Europe, for whom we are two human beings who take pleasure in adapting to the beauty and customs of a place that could quite easily have been the original garden of eden.

The CONFLENT TALES

Chapter the Nynth

The Wyfe of Eus's Tale Part 2

The Dénouement

The Wyfe of Eus's Tale

Well here I am. I'm back ! Bet you're glad to see me again after reading my first piece in Volume 1. I told my husband that 7000 words isn't enough for all I have to say – more like 70000, and that would be pushing it. So in Part 2, I'll try to give you some idea what's it's like to live here, just in case you fancy coming for a long visit, or to find a house in Paradise. There's so much to see and do. The first bit is for the ladies of course, though men are allowed to read it for the good of their souls.

Shopping in the Conflent

Shopping in France is often the starting point for a eulogy on the quaint customs and gastronomic delights to be found in the little village *alimentations;* the crusty incomparability of the bread from the *boulangerie;* the intellectually stimulating conversations one has with one's French butcher; the all-encompassing exoticism of the markets and so on. Alas, would it were so. Here in the real world of the Conflent, shopping is not really like that. The big bad world has closed in on us. True there are village *alimentations* and *boulangers* galore where customers can wait for hours while the shopkeeper discusses the state of her bunions with the client in front, and there is of course the all-encompassing exoticism of the Prades market.

Prades Market – a colourful extravaganza

But the truth is more prosaic than that. In the nearest metropolis of Prades (pop. 6000), most people shop at the supermarket, of which there are three in the vicinity. The twenty-first century has, for better or for worse, arrived in my little piece of France. Even the small food shops in the towns lay out their wares pick-it-up-yourself supermarket style, there is no longer the traditional customer-shopkeeper gossip on the local economy, the progress of Mme Touron's arthritis, the government's howling incompetence and the unbelievable price of children's clothes which used to be such a pleasant feature of French shopping. To compound the sin, many housewives also make a weekly or a monthly trip to the Perpignan hypermarkets, vast all-inclusive emporiums containing everything that can be eaten, drunk, worn, listened to, played with, sat upon, painted over, driven or stolen under one roof.

Personally, I obtain most of the weekly needs at the aptly named local Super-U in Prades, and this tends to satisfy most of my family's indulgences. Even though the value of our income sometimes takes a heavy battering from the fluctuations of the pound to the euro - we suffered a 25% reduction in the mid 1990s (this was the time of the *franc fort*) and a surplus more recently, thanks to the troubles of the Eurozone, until the illusional stupidity of the Brexit disaster plunged us back into penury - we find that, with careful financial husbandry and wifery, the cost of living compares well to that in the UK. That is, so long as we buy the things that are local and French. There is indeed a *section britannique* in Super U where one can buy such anglo-saxon delights as Heinz baked beans, Robertson's lime marmalade, Fray Bentos corned beef, Branston pickle, Marmite and the rest – just so long as one is prepared to pay through the nose for nostalgia. And if we were prepared to live off nothing but fruit during the long hot summers, we could virtually leave our purses in the drawer. That would have some messy consequences of course, and anyway I'm not inclined to give up my favourite pastime – my husband calls me the superwoman of the consumer society, and it's sure true that my need to shop is close to that of a junkie on crack-cocaine.

Conflent-speak

Nor is shopping language a problem for me. Supermarkets nowadays are international organisations and shopping is an international occasion, even though the extensive wine department in all the local supermarkets contains nothing but French wines and the local farmers frequently demonstrate against foreign imports from Spain by dumping their unsold peaches across the motorway. Come what may, I have little problem in ensuring that my needs are understood without the use of sign language. My husband's French is reasonably fluent, having had the benefit of seven years grammatical honing at his posh grammar school, after which he says he couldn't progress much further than *'Je.m'appelle'* as far as actual communication is concerned. He says Stratford-atte-Bowe would have been proud of him, whatever that means. As for me, a sec-mod product, I couldn't speak a word until I was 45, having been educated in an age (and it isn't that long ago) when gels who were not destined for university were considered to be nothing much more than kitchen fodder for potential husbands. But I'm a communicator. I spoke my first halting *'mon nom est Maggie'* five years ago during our first sojourn in Paris and haven't looked back since. Twenty-five years later I may not pass the audition as a potential newscaster for TF1, the main French TV channel, but I have little problem in making myself misunderstood in any company and in any language. The louder voices in our supermarkets are usually brits who seem to believe that the most effective way to overcome a problem of understanding is to double the decibels in their own language. Another method of overcoming loss of memory, or absence of vocabulary is to pronounce the English word as if it were also a French one. I frequently hear strangled expressions like *'Avez-vous du veendoffclenair'*, or *'ou sont les shoppeeng-basquettes?.'*

I introduce this subject of languages in the context of shopping to show how a superficial, nuance-free knowledge of language can backfire. In Britain we all know that preservatives are chemicals added to products in order to allow them to keep longer. We also know that some of them can be carcinogenic and, as an ex-nurse and a fervent environmentalist, I don't indulge in such products unless it's absolutely necessary, such as if I feel like committing suicide or murdering my husband (which happens often). Unfortunately a *preservatif* in French is not the same thing - as I am sure everyone except me would know, it is a condom. Thus on a recent visit to the supermarket, my husband will forever guard the touching picture of me waving a packet of fish soup and a tin of *petits pois a l'étuvée* at the shop assistant and asking her if they contained any preservatives. Shop assistants in this part of the world are resignedly accustomed to the peculiarities of the English, but this was a completely new angle for her. The idea that condoms should be immersed in a tin of peas, much less accompanying fish in a packet of soup, while not perhaps beyond the bounds of possibility, stretched the limits of her imagination. Being a well-brought up Catholic girl, her face, now the colour of a ripe Conflent peach, betrayed the conflicting emotions of guilt at the vividly clear picture now forming in her mind and fear that inner laughter would cause her to fold up in front of the mad customer. '*Er non, madame*, she stammered, face contorted, '*Il n'y en a pas!*', before she fled down the passage-way, presumably to search for the nearest white-coated man - or phone her boy-friend from the back room.

The Climatic Conflent

While preparing your holiday in this wonderful part of France, you will of course need to know about the sort of weather you can expect. We Brits tend to be a little obsessive about meteorology. And we have brought this paranoia to God's paradise on earth. To quote the geography books. the Conflent has a Mediterranean type climate, That isn't surprising since the said Mediterranean Sea is just half an hour down the road. And as I learned, even at my apology for a school, that means warm wet winters and hot dry summers. Don't believe a word of it. This is the only place I have been where I have suffered heat stroke while gardening in the middle of January. It is also the place where I have seen the most spectacular thunderstorms in August complete with hailstones the size of golf balls. These comprise extraordinary lightning effects with twin, triple and quadruple forks flashing across the valley and zapping the iron mines in the hills, thunder which can startle a deaf-mute and rain with no gaps in between. It is a mite difficult to generalise about weather in such an unpredictable place. In the Conflent it is of course tempered by the mountains. We are already at a thousand feet and climb very rapidly to nine thousand in the space of about five kilometres and so we have our very own microclimate. Such intense thunderstorms are to be expected in the summer not only because of geography, but also because the heat of the sun can become more than a little oppressive.

A typical August day would honour the starting gun with a beautifully clear sky and the sun beating down contentedly like a friendly yellow ball in the sky. The land, and the people on it, bask in its warmth like meerkats after a couple of gins and tonics. It then become progressively hotter until mid-afternoon when I could grill a pork chop on the window-sill – theoretically, of course, we normally use a barbecue. That's why we sometimes call this region the grilling fields. Sorree about that! Then, when the heat can be suffered no longer, the cumulo-nimbus with the black bits will draw up their battle-lines and worry the sun into hiding behind them. At this point it either rains or it doesn't - most of the time the latter, since the experience of real wet rain in these parts is a very local thing. It can be bucketing down next door and dry as Chicago under prohibition here. There are times, though, when the mould is broken and the entertainment programme includes celestial fireworks, complete with orchestral accompaniment and liquid evidence. This lasts for perhaps just over an hour before once again the sun has got his hat on and we shout hip hip hooray.

But little is typical in summer and we frequently experience long dreamy days of nothing but sunshine, torpor and rose wine. If – forgive me, when – you decide to come here, the Autumn is probably the best season of the year. For the most part the scenery is a painter's and photographer's delight - clear as a five dimensional picture and balmy as a forest glade. Such bliss normally lasts until mid-November and even at times into Christmas. I have been known to serve Christmas Dinner out on the patio. Granted we were wearing duffle coats and Balaclavas, our guests had doubled their underwear, and the turkey was served in the warm kitchen and transported to the table where it was eaten very quickly before it could freeze. But it was worth it just to make a point. Anyway where was I? Ah yes late December. After that the weeks pass, the nights become colder until by January we must reluctantly switch on our central heating or light our wood-burning stove, or both. These are the crystal clear nights when there seem to be more stars in the sky than gaps between them and the night temperatures go well below zero, 19 degrees below this year, creating a thick hoar frost for the morrow's sun to melt. January, February and March can be wet and cold at all times of the day, but equally we have known it to be as hot and steamy as Marilyn Monroe in these months. Snow comes our way one year in 3, and when it does the peach trees look like white lollipops ready for the Canigou to lick. Certainly the peach blossom seems to like the climate. Springtime is a delight. The hot sun dispels the winter darkness and the ever-longer days proclaim the ripe promise of another lazy, fruitful summer.

Winter Lollipop trees - February

Storm over the Conflent

But generalising about the Conflent weather is like gambling with the cards - a rogue hand can be dealt at any time. During the September of 1992, we were here for a two-week working holiday to batten down the hatches for a winter absence. It was the last weekend of the month and the time of the Prades show, and I was looking forward to attending our first encounter with the local pigs, cows and sheep there. The Friday morning was, as usual, bright and sunny. But around lunch-time the familiar dark, menacing cumulo-nimbus peered above the mountains on the horizon. Within minutes, a crepuscular pallor pervaded the earth and oppressed the air as the day gradually assumed the garb of night, until we were forced to illume the lights in the house. My husband drove me slowly through this eerie scene into Prades on full headlights, so dark was it at two in the afternoon. As we disembarked from our car to enter the Catena shop the first few spots of rain began to fall. Then, suddenly and with an audible gasp, the sky opened the sluicegates. Within seconds it was as if we were standing under the Niagara falls. The roads were transmuted into rivers, the water disposal system being totally inadequate to deal with such quantities of instant liquid. In the two yards we had to run to get in the car from the shop door we were soaked to our bones. It was impossible to drive anywhere since the fast-flowing torrent in the roadway was at wheel height and quickly spreading laterally into the houses and shops. It was still as black as the blackest night as the rain eased a little and allowed us to drive slowly and carefully down the Prades to Eus road into our little *chemin*, over the swirling waters just under the bridge, and back to the *mas*. As we garaged the car, the deluge recommenced with renewed ferocity. The water would have bounced back three feet if it had been allowed to but such was the weight of falling downpour it could not bounce at all. Lightning flashed but it could not be seen, thunder crackled and could not be heard.

I changed and donned my golfing waterproofs, raised my trusty golf umbrella and walked back along the lane. Within one minute the protection was as nothing, I was once again a sodden creature of the day-night. I approached the bridge over the stream and saw through the gloom what I had never expected to see - no bridge, just a rushing wall of water where the bridge had been. We were effectively cut off from civilisation. So, now trembling with apprehension, I retraced my route back to the *mas* and crept gingerly down the steps to the stream, torch in hand. It was 3 p.m and Watermans could not have choreographed the inky blackness better. At the seventh step, I felt my feet under water, looked down and saw the roaring torrent just one foot below. The stream, one of the few escape routes from the pluvial battering on the Canigou mountain, had risen 15 feet in one hour. If anyone mentions the phrase 'flash flood' in future I have an exact image in my mind. To have fallen into it would have resulted almost certainly in a watery death. I retreated back to the house. From the balcony we all watched through the gloom the adjacent meadow disappear under the swirling waters and thought thoughts of evacuation, worried that the house, a full forty feet above the stream might eventually succumb. But evacuate where to? - we were the highest point in the vicinity. An anxious evening ensued as the din of the relentless battering penetrated the thick house walls. It banged and clattered on the roof, threatening to smash in the skylight and engulf us all. The electricity flickered constantly but, mercifully, did not fail us. Around eleven pm we crept into bed wondering whether we should be dressed in pyjamas or swimming costumes or wetsuits.

The fury lasted the sleepless night long, remorselessly attacking from above, hour after hour, wave after wave of merciless fluid battalions seeking out every weakness in our defences. It abated only with the call of the dawn. We emerged timidly like mice from a tiny hole to survey the damage. The morning sun beamed brilliantly down pretending that nothing had happened. Only the scene of devastation showed the traces of the previous day's adventures. It was not as bad as it might have been, but nor was it a pretty sight. Trees with a diameter of five and six feet had simply disappeared from sight, the meadow was still half under water, the rest a sea of oozing mud, the bridge had survived the onslaught, the stream had halted some feet below the house. And, as William Wordsworth might have said if he hadn't been seduced by the French Revolution at the time, bliss was it in that dawn to be alive and surviving, which is more than can be said for the Prades show, which was due to start on that day..

So much for the balmy weather of Autumn. I talked of this to our farmer neighbour, he of the best peaches in the world. With a gallic shrug, he dismissed the whole event as if it were an everyday occurrence. *'Ca arrive toutes les dix années'* he said nonchalantly, but the twinkle in his eye betrayed him. Every ten years it might have been but he too had been impressed, and perhaps even a little bit troubled.

The windy Conflent

The last item on the subject of climate has to be the *tramontane*, the wind which blows from the North and North-East and terrorises the neighbourhood like a force five hurricane in the gulf. I mentioned it before in my first literary incarnation in volume 1. In winter it is, like the *mistral,* bitterly cold and in summer it warms a little, rather like a reluctant virgin. The locals have accustomed themselves to its outrages. They say it always blows for an odd number of days one, three, five or seven and though I haven't counted, I always accept as gospel any folklore we are told. They haven't got round to the subject of little green men yet, but tales of the green lizards abound. They are said to bring luck. There is one in my garden and I call it Oscar, though a small rockfall in his stony habitat might have seen him off. Whatever, back to the wind. The *tramontane* is usually strong - it has been known to blow in excess of 100 miles an hour and in winter it rattles our lounge windows mercilessly. In order to ease the pressure on the glass I open them a little, so that on *tramontane* days the house sounds like a scene from a Hammer film. It frightens the animals to death. Its howling and shrieking and wailing are like the sound effects from the scene in Wuthering Heights where Cathy shouts for Heathcliffe. Here, many houses are built into the lee of the hills in order to achieve some shelter from its icy blast, but our m*as*, being *en plein campagne*, right in the middle of the Prades plain, gets the full force of its attention. It is the *tramontane* which gives the Conflent a reputation for windiness, but I have to say that, once I have habituated myself to it, even a seven day blow gives me little discomfort. At the time of writing, August, I have felt neither puff nor blow of any of the Greek Anemoi for at least two months.

1001 Musical Nights

The problem of food for the body seems to have been cracked for us in the Conflent. But what if you are worried about the equally important matter of sustenance for mind and soul? One of the drawbacks of living in such a remote part of a foreign country might be a lack of accessible culture, theatre, art, music, for my husband and me, raw materials for a full and fulfilled life. Music is our particular *passion.* We have a fairly catholic range of musical tastes, with a preference for the jazz and the classical. I thought that we would have to assuage the absence of live symphonic and operatic stimulation through our wide range of DVDs and CDs. How wrong we were. No music? I am absolutely overwhelmed by a prodigality of the stuff. In the summer season the opportunities explode exponentially. Every village and town competes with every other for its ration of money-spending tourists and the months of July and August are saturated with assorted concerts and other events in churches and abbeys, in village halls, in private houses, in castle grounds, in the open air, in the public toilets for all we know.

Take the annual Prades music festival. It is famous world-wide. It originated 50 years ago through the influence of the town's then most famous inhabitant, Pablo Casals, a world-class cellist and a former refugee from Franco's Spain, who laid down his heart and his domicile in the town. The small museum to his name in the *Office de Tourisme* records how deeply he was loved by the people, and Prades still has a flourishing *école de musique* based around the Casals festival. For the most part this is a chamber music extravaganza - but each year a major choral and instrumental work will raise the roof of the church of St Pierre in Prades. Last year it was the Haydn Creation, superbly sung by choirs and orchestra from all over Southern France. The assembled multitude of performers was so numerous that there was little room for an audience. The chamber concerts are somewhat pricy but then the mayor has to have his cut, and this is, after all, high-class euphony. Most of the world's best have performed in its real home, the exquisite 9th century cloistered Abbey of *St Michel de Cuxha* on the road to the pretty village of Taurinya. This year two visiting critics from the Sunday Telegraph took up temporary residence at the *mas* of our friends and described it as the best chamber music they had heard for many years. The festival stirs the town into life from the end of July to the middle of August. But it isn't all cerebral etherealism. For those with more popular tastes the *place* resonates on 4 evenings of the summer weeks with rock groups, coblas, jazz trios, dance-bands and individual musical talent displays. More of that later.

But Prades is not the only place to bring music to our ears. The massive organ built in the 18th century by a certain Jean-Pierre Cavaillon, long-forgotten except for organ enthusiasts, in the *église St Joseph* at Vinça down the road is the justification for receiving a subvention from the regional culture fund. It also serves as an excuse for organising concerts in a fascinating mixture of music in the church there. Choirs from as far away as Barcelona, Paris, Montpellier and Cambridge have given marvellous performances here, as well as soloists, instrumentalists, wind quartets, organists and Patagonian nose-flute players – well, maybe not the last one but again maybe I missed that one. One particularly superb programme of

16th century motets, Negro spirituals and delicately-scored popular songs by a group called the Cambridge Scholars stands out in our minds. At the end, as the singers returned for what seemed the fifteenth time and gave their tenth encore, I remember one unmistakably Irish voice shouting out from the middle of the congregation 'Just sing Danny Boy like that one more time *please* and I'll die happy'.

Some 20 kilometres away in the hills, in the village of Mosset, they go one further by organising an opera festival each year. Such operatic favourites as The Barber of Seville, Carmen, Man of La Mancha, and, this year, a superb performance of the Magic Flute, have resonated within the courtyard of the roofless castle at the top of the village. The chorus was composed of warblers from the local choirs, while world-class soloists were imported from all over the globe by Albert, a local Dutchman with all the right contacts. For nine nights a packed audience sat in hushed silence as Tamino, Papageno, Zoroaster et al held them spellbound, and the Queen of the Night coloratura'ed her way through the arpeggios. My husband said that he had seen the Flute performed several times in major cities all over the world, San Francisco, Melbourne, Brisbane, Prague, London etc, and yet this one in a village of 250 people out in the sticks of the high Conflent was as good as any he had experienced. The audience are in no way opera buffs. Indeed their knowledge of it is similar to my knowledge of Sanskrit, but they turn up in their droves and are spell-bound for a night.

In our own small village of Eus another eight concerts, mostly of Catalan music, are planned every year by an outfit called the Boris Vian Foundation (Boris is the guy who brought Jazz to France, wrote surrealist books and hung about the Boulevard St Germain with his cronies – Jean-Paul Sartre and Simone de Beauvoir. His widow emigrated here from Paris many aeons ago). While some of them are of the avant-garde fruitcake variety, others have provided memorable moments to savour, especially the top-class jazz evenings.

Ille-sur-Têt, a town ten kilometres away, organises one-off concerts at all times of year and we have only touched the tip of the musical iceberg. Perpignan, forty kilometres away, is a venue for annual jazz, big band and orchestral festivals and, during the winter, free weekly concerts given by visiting musicians to the University's music department. On every Thursday of July and August the pavements of all parts of the city resonate to the sounds of jazz, pop, flutes, violins, saxophones, throat pipes and the most maniacal drummers to be seen East of Nashville.

In the next valley, easily reachable in half-an-hour, the musical tradition is even stronger. The tiny village of Rasiguères might not be a name on every builder's lips but the cognoscenti will know that in the early 1970s it was a favourite haunt of the then British Prime Minister, Edward Heath and the celebrated concert pianist Moura Lympany. The village even named its finest wine vintages after them. The cuvée Moura Lympany is one of the best rosé wines of the area and the cuvée Edward Heath an excellent red, the colour of his face when he spoke about Mrs Thatcher. Since, like Edward Heath, they have been discontinued since the early 80s, the labels are, unlike him, in great demand. The Rasiguères International Music Festival was synonymous with high quality for almost twenty years, but it went into decline by 1990 and now no longer exists. However, *plus ca change plus c'est la même chose*. The cavalry, led by John Bethell, a former BBC man, rode into Latour de France, another village 10 kilometres down the road from Rasiguères. This year marked the 12th international festival of arts and music of Latour de France. It entertains the locals and anyone else who chooses to turn up for one week at the end of July and attracts every year more than a hundred amateur chorists from all parts of Lancashire and the Isle of Man. With them come some of the best solo voices England can muster, a guest concert pianist (this year, Clive Lythgoe) and a brass group which plays, or rather enforces, a wide range of music all over the village, reaching the places other festival parts don't reach.

For a whole week they make enthusiastic international music, singing, playing, performing, in the square, on the rooftops, in the sewers, in the courtyards of houses, in the church. It is a feast of melody, capped by a blockbuster oratorio on the last night. The conductor, soloists and choir are cheered until the church is in danger of shaking down and everyone goes home every night musically satiated and deliriously happy. Last year, at my instigation, a youth brass band from Tyldesley, not a million miles from my birthplace in Lancashire, made a foray to Eus and enchanted a *grande foule* in the Eus village hall. Youngsters from 5 to 15 played solos and band favourites on the terrace of the village hall against the backdrop of a mellow Canigou. It was, as usual, a magical evening. As a post-concert reward, Michele, the Mayor's wife, and her helpers commandeered the *Maison du temps libre* kitchen and delivered unto them a catalan meal of gluttonous proportions accompanied by generous quantities of much-appreciated local wine - trumpet and tuba playing create an uncommon thirst in spectators, the children being too young for such delights, at least in the sight of their minders. The feast continued until 2 am, whereupon some of the brass group took out their instruments and gave a special concert for the Mayor, who had not been able to attend the concert. Those villagers who had missed out the first time became a willing or unwilling audience on the second. Of such moments are great memories made. The only references to the noise from the villagers the following day were all congratulatory - they had listened too. We doubt that that would have happened in England.

Other brass groups from the same source have made a similar impression. The following year Brass Equale, an Isle of Man group, produced sounds seldom heard in the Eus church and enthralled both the live audience and probably the dead one beneath the stones, though we didn't hear them join in the applause.

Equale brass band playing in front of the Eus church altar-piece

John Bethell relates a tale of the first Latour de France festival, when he was approached by a strange Frenchman while quaffing a beer in the village square. In halting English he was asked if he was Mr Bethell, to which he replied in the affirmative. 'Ah', said the man, 'You will be interested in the opera house I *have chez moi.*' 'Indeed' says John, trying to hide that he was humouring the man. '*Ah oui*' he said ' It is not far from here, would you like to see it?' Trapped! So, in order not to give offence to this very pleasant madman, John agreed to accompany him to *chez lui*. He was led to a large but unprepossessing mansion on the edge of the village and through iron gates into the garden and eventually into the house. 'Come and see my library' said the stranger, whereupon he opened a concealed door in one of the panels of the hall and stepped into a 60 seater late eighteenth century opera chamber. It was exquisite, untouched since that time except that round its periphery were bookcases full of antique books. The place had been built *à l'époque* by a well-known singer from the Paris opera who had retired to the area and wanted to celebrate her triumphs. He was gobsmacked. The opportunity to restore such a gem to its rightful purpose and conduct in it overwhelmed him. 'But monsieur' he said 'this must be used in the festival we are giving here in Latour'. 'Ah non, Monsieur' said the man 'That would not be possible, it is my Library'. And so it has stayed to this day. John tells the tale convincingly and well and, despite our expressions of disbelief, he rigidly maintains the truth of it.

On the road which winds up from Ille-sur-Têt to Belesta in the hills, there is another larger mansion on the hillside. Behind it, on top of a knoll, is a large mausoleum built in the form of an ark. It is the final resting place of yet another 19th century doyen of the Paris opera. I don't know what it is about this area which attracts old divas to come here to die, but perhaps it is another reflection of the rich musical heritage which survives and thrives to this day.

Do it yourself music

At the risk of boring you with my enthusiasm for music – this will be the last word, honest. We don't always have to be entertained. During the long winter months we often make our own musical performances. Our part in the infamous Eus choir will be fully documented in another chapter but our frequent dinner parties are punctuated by what might euphemistically be called bursts of song, usually retro – very retro. To describe it as music might be over-exaggeration but it's indicative of a desire, even a strategy of sorts, though with a lamentable absence of implementation skills, to lighten the long winter nights.

I lied. There is just one more and then I'll drop the subject. On the first Sunday of every month from October to June there are meetings of *'les amis de la musique'*, a franco-british group of music-lovers who gather in each others' homes to share harmonious experiences. I, together with my husband, am the President. Not every woman can call herself President! The programme is always that of whoever is hosting the event. They decide what shall be heard and usually put a theme to it. Thus last year we had, among others, the music of Schostakovich, a selection of big-band sounds, a capella choral works, an evening of Jazz guitar and a history of Concertos, Cadenzas and Codas with examples from Bach to Berg given by yours truly. Each concert, presented in French and English includes an intermission during which samples of the wines of the region are taken and, after the final coda, the sampling continues if enough people have been able to stay awake. Usually the 'amis' season starts with a live soirée in which the patrons are invited to enter into the spirit of things by dressing as Victorian, or French Third Empire, as they can. This is not obligatory and, in view of the heat in September, probably not medically recommended. We have some wonderful voices in this area, our friends Jo and Helen being both trained operatic performers and both having access to other local musicians. These soirées try to reproduce the Victorian drawing room image, though the singing is of a much higher quality than the stereotype.

The season always finishes in June with a Glyndebourne-type afternoon complete with champagne etc on the lawn of one of our members with a big enough garden. Pretentious? Us? Surely not. There are neither hospitality boxes nor live performances but the experience is always greatly appreciated by our French friends. The real Glyndebourne ambiance is evoked when it rains, as has happened the last two years.

In between these formal meetings, visiting celebrities are enthusiastically enjoined to demonstrate their talents at impromptu concerts. Last year, when the son and daughter in law of our nearest English neighbours came to visit - they were principal baritone and soprano at the Eisenach opera company – the standard reflex action was to organise a concert *chez Jo* with some of the university musicians and the celebrated local organist and pianist, Pierre Vidal. And so we did. It was a special evening with singing and playing of the highest quality in the privacy of Jo's own home, except in the last item when my husband and I gave a somewhat unharmonious – well the wine *had* flowed like a river in spate - rendering of 'All in the April Evening' simply to emphasise how superb the others really were. So passes my musical year, a constant round of blissful experiences of which Polyhymnia, the musing daughter of Mnemosyne, would be proud.

Water, water .....

But she wouldn't be proud of the water music. Tales of land disputes are rare in this valley, but when it comes to the question of water, then all reason has to be abandoned. Marcel Pagnol's classic novels *Jean de Florette* and *Manon des Sources*, both turned into films, tell an accurate story of greed and intrigue around this liquid gold, even though situated elsewhere in France. The importance of water is etched into every peasant brain, a race memory of centuries of drought and inter-family wars over the precious stuff. Even in these days of barrages, careful dissemination and relative plenty, water is the source of disputes and confrontations. The complex system of canals, irrigation channels and ditches delivering water to every field and meadow is said to have been mostly in place by the 14th century, though the raw material to feed them has not always been there. It is a simple but effective system not unlike the levadas of Madeira. Large canals, fed by the river Têt, wind their way around the valley contours like elongated snakes. From these, the farmers raise the sluice gates which feed their own fields, themselves a complex pattern of sluices and *vannes,* and take their weekly ration at preset times. Having watered the fields and inundated the land, the excess runs back into the canal lower down or back into the river. It is a simple iterative water feedback system and it is jealously guarded. Suspicious farmers used to stand watch on each other and make sure that not one thimbleful of illegitimate liquid was extracted from the canal, a bit like stake jumping in the gold rush. They are more relaxed in these times of plenty but some still retain the old habits. Our neighbour has more than once been threatened with death by a whole family of agriculteurs, carrying, in time-honoured rural fashion, pitchforks, for mistakenly opening the wrong sluicegate.

Friendly natives

Which brings me to our relationships with the natives of this green and pleasant land. For your visit I guess that you will want to know if they are friendly or not. After all, if you think that you are going to be placed in a pot and stewed with the peaches you may not be the most eager visitor to our region. So here's a little tale that answers that question.

So predictable is the summer weather here in the Conflent that I can usually work out when it is a good day to take a picnic. I do this often with our visitors if only because it gets me out of the kitchen into the fresh mountain air. Our favourite spot is at Marcevol, a 10th century working priory on the hills above the village. Here there is flat land, protection from the wind if needed and an interesting monument with its own simple message of timelessness. We took our Wigan friends Bill and Sue up there last year. Unfortunately the tramontane was making its presence felt and the lee-land behind the abbey was already taken by about 30 families who had brought tables, chairs and their own grilling machinery. No matter, what wind there was was not exactly blowing off the mountain, and so we parked our bums on a blanket on the ground further down the hill – our level of picnic sophistication knows no bounds - and laid out our goodies ready to tuck in. Five minutes later an emissary from the party came down and offered us sausages from their grill, which we accepted with lots of bonhomie and gratitude. Much preferable to corned beef butties. Another five minutes, another one came bearing wine and indicated that if we would like to join in the party, we would be very welcome to do so. Since our friends spoke no French and they no English we declined as gracefully as possible in the circumstances and explained why. This reason was graciously accepted. But they said, 'even if you will not join us will you partake of our food. The pork chops are now ready.'

What an invitation! We could no longer play the parts of the stand-offish English and we accepted on condition that our meagre offerings of butties and pork pies were put into the ring. Done, they said, and so we joined the merry party which just getting into its full swing. It turned out that they were a party of former paratroopers who had seen action in the North African desert and they brought their families to this spot every year on this day for their annual get-together. When they learned that Bill and my husband had spent some national service time in the RAF, however compulsory and undesired, we were bosom pals forever, despite the corned beef sandwiches which lay uneaten on a plate near the fire. Dave, my husband and the paratroopers exchanged, as macho males will, tales of audacious heroism, they of aerial campaigns in the desert, our heroes of spud-bashing campaigns in the canteen; they of stoicism and bravery in the face of enemy fire, our pissartists of courage and endurance in the face of sergeants and square-bashing sadists. The bond was forged and we were invited to join in the next year and the year after that into perpetuity, and not only to bash the spuds. We women too made excellent progress, inventing new forms of sign-language not previously known to womankind, like a gaggle of deaf-mutes on laughing gas. We had a whale of a time. We often ask ourselves whether this would have happened in the UK, where strangers tend to be treated with suspicion and the group fortress mindset is much stronger. Perhaps it would, but no-one could have been friendlier than these ancient French combatants who wished to offer their own gratitude for Britain's part in liberating their country.

Health and beauty in the Conflent

This chapter about living in the Conflent would not be complete without some observations about health and health care. Heaven forfend that you should become ill while here, but the following story should put your anxious mind at rest. When my husband took early retirement it came with a health package. Private health insurance, it said, would not be available to him in France until he reached the age of 63. Meanwhile, he should initially claim what was available from the French National Health Service. Unluckily for him, he's a walking chemistry set. He needs pills, potions and poisons for several maladies he'd rather not have but is unfortunately stuck with for the rest of his life. He's not infirm or likely to kick the bucket at any time, you understand - at least not more than any one of us - but he's a fairly high risk character medically speaking and his essential potions amounted to more than 150 euros per month. Drugs are expensive in these parts, though not half as expensive as they are in the UK.

After he attained the ripe old age of 65, a baby nowadays, there was no problem. There is a reciprocal medical treaty between Britain and France to re-imburse people of retirement age wherever they may be in those countries. Similarly with me. Before 65 it was wise to remain healthy. The first thing one learns in this situation is that, unlike our Dutch, German and Scandinavian colleagues, British-style medical care for Brits living abroad is limited to a short period which doesn't often exceed more than 2 years. After that one is expected to insure oneself. But of course, no insurance company in its right mind will cover the costs of expensive drugs. Nor will they cover primary care like visits to the doctor for which one has to pay in this country. British insurance companies are most reluctant to pay out for anything and the French ones will not take the risk at all, especially for an *etranger*.

So the prospective settler in France *d'un certain age* needs to think very carefully before upping sticks and plunging into the French countryside. No-one is going to pay for expensive medicines you may need and no-one wants to pay for routine visits to the doctor. If you are younger and taking a job, or older and beyond retirement age, there is no problem. Likewise if you are a visitor. Once you are in the French social security system the treatment is superb, the best in the world according to the World Health Organisation. The Conflent heaves with spas and recuperation centres, as one might expect in an area so beautiful, and the standard of medical provision is as right as a perfect apple. If you do not come into those categories, you have been warned.

But now, having reached the magic age, we are both well and truly esconced in the system, and it is as well that we are. My husband's liver is a world-class factory for the manufacture of low-quality cholesterol and his blood is, or at least was, a teeming river of fatty plaques. Ten years ago his body, and his cardiologist, delivered the chilling message that it was time for a heart by-pass or three. At the same time the echograph discovered a kink in his renal artery that was depriving his left kidney of the sustenance it needed to survive. A double life-threatening whammy. So there he was in the day clinic digesting the news, when the doctor asked him how soon he wanted to put the problems right, a question not often asked in the British health service where waiting lists for heart surgery were at the time stretching into the far future. Indeed Bill, our Wigan friend mentioned earlier, had been on such a list for already 18 months. He gave the obvious answer 'as soon as possible.' 'Right' they said ' we'll do the stent in the renal artery this afternoon and let you recover from that for ten days, then we'll do the by-pass.' We were both gobsmacked. He wasn't even given time to contemplate the implications for mortality, let alone re-draw his will, before they had him in a white gown on the trolley on the way to the theatre to straighten out the kink. And sure enough, ten days later he was once more dressed as a vestal virgin praying before the butchers in the hospital carvery. That's efficiency! But there is more. Instead of sending him home with a list of exercises to do and foods to eat as happens in Britain, he was whisked off to a recuperation centre for 4 weeks where the resident physiotherapists jolly well made sure he did the necessary to ensure a complete recovery. Two months later he was on the first tee at Marcevol Golf club, while Bill was just then preparing to meet his maker in a British hospital. Thankfully, Bill's maker allowed him some more time after the op, but the difference between the two systems is clear.

Back to rights

At the risk of pushing the health story too far again, I'll finish with another tale of the operating theatre. Two years after these momentous incidents, my own back finally gave up the ghost, the lumbar disks having by then all but disappeared. It started when I visited the doc because my back was playing rhythmic tunes to an accompaniment of mainly percussion instruments. A few x-rays later I was referred to a surgeon in Montpellier to ask how 3 of my discs seemed to have vanished from the map of my lumbar region. 'I can rebuild you', he said. 'We have ways of making you well, but it will involve long, delicate and expensive surgery if you are willing to subject yourself to my knives and scalpels'. 'Do your worst', replied I apprehensively, 'My confidence in your surgical skills surpasses all reason.' And it did. Hence the month before the surgery was taken up by a series of preparatory exercises to strengthen both my back and my will. The fateful day arrived. Dressed in the obligatory virginal white robe, I was wheeled into the theatre of the Clinique du Parc in Montpellier, there to be anteriorily opened up while the mysterious doctor by-passed aorta and other vital organs to insert 3 tiny titanium discs into my lumbar spine. That certainly put paid to any movement for the next week. Meanwhile my husband was anxiously holding off another putative heart attack in a nearby hotel. Success! Part 1 was completed without a hitch and so a week later he turned me over, revealed the posterior vertebrae, scraped out the osteoarthritic residue of the years, performed 2 laminectomies, released the spinal nerves and fitted a flexible arthrodese while he was at it. All of this, as you may guess, had a deleterious effect on my Scottish Country Dancing prospects for the rest of the year. The next month was spent often encased in the hard plastic version of an 'iron lady', in a *centre de re-education*' similar to that my husband had endured – bouts of intense boredom alleviated by encounters with muscular physiotherapists, selected instruments of physical torture and canteen offerings euphemistically described as food, a survival course of epic intensity. Four years further on, my born again back is like that of a young girl

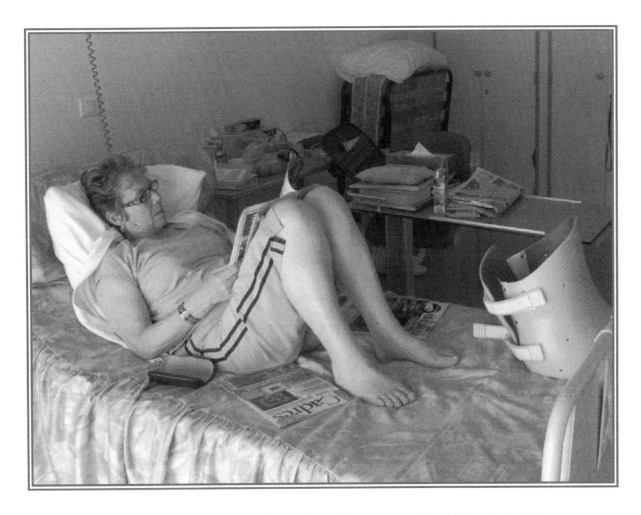

Bouts of intense boredom often encased in a 'Plastic Lady'

What these two tales tell us is that, while life might be a lottery, we are far more likely to buy the right tickets here in France. Indeed, as we, and the WHO, have already said, France is regarded as world number 1 in the health contest, while Britain comes in at number 18 (and the US at number 25). So, barring a major family catastrophe or an earthquake in the Pyrennees, we're staying put thank you very much.

On returning to my Pyrennean civilisation, I was commanded to take it easy, to eschew stress and to leave everything to my husband. Normally my husband is to cooking, cleaning and gardening what elephants are to ballet dancing, but, needs must, he became head chef, chief *homme de ménage*, top gardener, principal nurse, elected dog-walker and president of the Maggie get well campaign, posts he continued to hold for as long as I could pretend to be mortally wounded.

Readers can make their own comparisons about health care but we think we are in the right place for aging. And all of this was for free to us. The titanium disks glow brightly on the X-rays like three milky ways. They send the airport scanners crazy, and that's a problem in this day and age of suicide bombers and belligerent security guards. But the surgeons in Britain, and even in the USA, are only now hesitantly contemplating similar operations for chronic back sufferers, while I now dance and leap about like a reborn teenager – well, a reasonably docile one anyway.

As I write now, all of this is in great jeopardy. The dimwitted loonies who voted for Brexit and the termination of our way of life (as well of that of almost 2 million other British ex-pats) have more or less destroyed our entitlement to the wonders of French health care. Our 25 years of residence in the European Union may allow us to stay here in our dotage but access to the French health system without paying a ransom is in doubt. For millions of British, the gate to the delights of Europe has been firmly closed, mainly by flag-waving, gullible, manipulated older people who would rather ruin their own economy than see their fellow brits happy in another land. It's the kids I feel sorry for. No longer will they be able to study, settle, open their minds and find a job within the wider embrace of a United Europe. And believe me, jobs will be scarce in Britain if the exodus of industry in search of a wider marketplace continues as it is doing now. I will say no more on this subject but, now that we are both in our 80s, it concerns us greatly.

Joos and the wedding

Anyway, back to something jollier. It is inappropriate to leave a chapter on living in the Conflent on such a sombre note so let me relate a story about my Dutch friend, Joos, in the village. He is in fact my husband's tennis partner in inter-club matches and his name is in fact Joosens, but that is unrecognisable down here, so Joos he has become.

Once again this is a story about the careless and innocent use of language. The French tend to have at least two meanings for words - one normal and one raunchy. Some 15 years ago Joos's daughter came to live in the village and fell in love with a French boy. The courtship went well and so, in the blissful anticipation of many pleasant days visiting their daughter, their new son in law and the future issue of their union, her parents bought them a house here.

The two youngsters were duly married. An enormous wedding ceremony took place in the village, attended by the great, the good and the familiar from the region and, it seemed, half of Holland as well. Heroic was the devouring and tippling, loud was the tumult of intoxicated voices, and happy were the new proclamations of undying entente between Holland and

France. Maastricht - that is the 17th century siege of by Vauban, the self-same who also built Villefranche up the road - was forever consigned to the dustbin of historical aberration.

As is the tradition in France, as well as in England, it came the turn for the bride's father to make his speech. The whole hall hushed in expectancy, since Joos is a well-known public speaker of some accomplishment. His face bright red and rosy from the wine, he raised his hands in the air in the manner of Christ blessing the multitude, and gave the awaiting assembly his broadest smile. *'Je jouit'* he trumpeted loudly and triumphantly, thinking it meant I rejoice, which in normal circumstances it does. And then he paused for dramatic effect.

He got it. Half the hall, the French half, exploded in barely silent laughter, while the Dutch half looked around at the French and at each other in confused bewilderment. Joos was non-plussed. He had deliberately chosen this first welcoming salvo for maximum effect as a springboard for his next dramatic utterance and the reaction from the audience was not at all what he had anticipated. Nevertheless, like the experienced trooper he was he continued through the French sniggers and the Dutch silence. Joos only discovered the secret of the laughter after the event. Apparently the other French meaning of the word is 'I am having an orgasm.'

So now you know more about this Elysium called the Conflent. And you know why I think that it is the most exquisite, wonderful, delightful, magnificent, marvelous, beautiful place in the whole world. I hope that you have been convinced enough to call in and see it for yourself. Maybe this poem, written by my husband, the ymmygrant, will help. Bye

The Coming

We came my wife the dog and I
To seek our fortune one July
We travelled south right to the med
Because we had it in our head
That here we' d find a sunny sky

We found ourselves a new domain
Where la belle France meets macho Spain
Adjacent to the Pyrennees
Where nature's beauty serves to please
We settled in our new terrain

Forty minutes from the sea,

Forty minutes from the ski
Plain centre of a fertiile vale
We found the perfect house for sale
Artur, Maggie and me, we three

Three storeys reach up to the sun
There's room enough for everyone
The seasons come, the seasons go, t
The summer heat, the winter snow
Pears and peaches by the ton

Mountains where the eagles soar
Can all be seen from our front door
A garden where the flowers grow,
Fruit trees in a summer glow
The sunsets are to murder for

The views are fashioned to entice
This truly is a paradise
Here we are and here we stay,
Here we work and here we play
The ambiance is beyond price

Far away from tabloid smear
We like the sun, we like the beer

Our former stress is now quite dead,
With joyful heart and serene head
There is no going back from here

The dog is happy once again
No more walkies in the rain
If you'd like to see the view,
We'll share our Shangri-la with you
Just bring a bottle of champagne

The Conflent Tales

Chapter the Tenth

The Scottysh Country Dancer's Tale

Being the story of how an alien dance culture insinuated itself into la France profonde

The Scottish Country Dancer's Tale

It may come as something of a shock to hear that an epidemic of Scottish Country Dancing has broken out in the middle of la France Profonde. But there's a simple explanation and, this time, the auld alliance is not to blame. Quite frankly most of the Catalans confess to a total ignorance of any such mac-kinship, partly because this part of the world was Spanish at the time it was being forged, and mostly because Mary Queen of Scots might just as well be an aging rock star for all they know. In other words they are as interested in Scottish History as much as the average Aberdonian is interested in the Spanish Civil War. The Conflent has a knack of distancing itself from the rest of the world and immersing itself in the bubble of its own Catalan cultural traditions, for example hunting any animal that moves or bird that flies into virtual extinction, multiplying by two the French statistics for death on the roads and, as the immigrant has said, dancing the Sardane at every opportunity.

My name's Hamish by the way, and as you may deduce, I'm one of Scottish diaspora. When my wife and I first came to this promised land, we were the only permanent British outcasts in our village. We thought we were unique, the only ones to escape from the frantic Hell that was, and still seems to be, Britain, to a more tranquil, serene and superior way of life. Tell us we were running away if you like and maybe you have a point, though we are not alone in our self-administered exile. But the solitary lotus-eating was not to last very long. Within a year the exodus from John Major's back-to-basics heaven had started in earnest and four other brit families came to install themselves inside a mile of our four-bed, two bath hermitage. We began to wonder if some latter day Aaron had parted the waters between Calais and Dover to allow the tribes of Britannia to cross. Since that time, the waters have little to do with the emigration. Low cost airlines, specifically Ryanair and Flybe flights to Perpignan, have opened up the flood-gates. Each successive year, the yearning to experience the good life in a French Paradise, preferably as far away as possible from Blair's, Brown's and Cameron's Britain, has continued through summer and winter, the frenzy slowed down only by the trivial matter of a global financial crisis. Undeterred by flight departure times that make a lark look like Rip Van Winkle, eager day-trippers and curious grockels board the daily flying tube in order to see the sights and inspect the curious habits and customs of this corner of their neighbour's real estate.

Some of them even tear themselves from the beaches to explore the mountains of the hinterland. They discover our beautiful Conflent and they like what they see. The result is an invasion of *étrangers* and an exponential hike in local house prices to levels undreamed-of by the indigenous peasantry. These proud people are not too proud to flog uncle Pascal's leaking old barn to the idiots who, much to their astonishment, want to pay huge sums to own it.

For us it's a mixed blessing. To have one's primary residence valued at 12 times its purchase price in 20 years is a dubious pleasure, when so many young people can now no longer afford to buy their own first home. To make matters worse, so many of the British and Dutch incomers leave their houses unlived in for long periods of the year that we are wondering when the local people will borrow a leaf from the Welsh nationalist hymn-book and take more direct action. But that's another story to be told later.

Of course we early pioneers all came here to integrate into a new culture. Of course we intended to avoid other Brits as if they were infected with the black death. And of course we are all astounded and disturbed that others have intruded on our territory to share our Shangri-La. Or are we? It seems that human nature is not like that. It takes the line of least resistance. It is so much easier to speak one's native language, than to flounder helplessly in one that gave so much trouble in one's youth. O level French may have its advantages, but actually speaking the language was not one of its more obvious outcomes.

And here in our village, ex-patriate brits all appear to have similar tales to tell, similar backgrounds to reveal, similar interests to share and similar parties to attend. There are for example the noisy and maniacal *soirées* to which we treat both our group of friends and our neighbours, always taking care to warn the latter and to invite them in advance. After the first time, somehow they always find something else to do, preferably several miles away, and never do they admit to having heard our efforts to awake the sleeping Canigou with a song. And we are versatile. Among the village *britanniques* our talents range from gourmet Chinese cooking to vegetable growing, from opera singing to environmental protection, from poetry-writing to cherry-stoning, from nursing care to teaching English as a foreign language. Friends and acquaintances in the other local villages have a similarly wide range of talents. The Conflent is a thriving university of ex-patriate expertise and knowledge, so powerful as to revive a modern-day missionary spirit disguised in the current jargon as 'integration into the community.'

Which brings me, in an oblique way, to the Conflent Scottish Country Dancing Society. In this other mountainous land of the South, we have our fair share of Scots, including myself, who suffered the school-time dance lessons in our long-ago previous lives. Strange how time and wisdom seems to leaven an embarrassing and unloved experience into something infinitely more desirable. Even more how distance tends to lend a peculiar enchantment to reeling the Duke of Argyll, jigging the posties, waltzing with St Bernard and other long-forgotten delights. Even the Gay Gordons, which in my day was a dance rather than an opportunity for a snigger, has its attractions. There's no accounting for the abnormalities of the human psyche.

And so we formed a Scottish Country Dancing Society, meeting monthly at our small, and now small and bewildered, village hall. Each third Sunday during the winter a curious mixture of the displaced, disoriented and dysfunctional gather together to man and womanhandle the pride of Scotland's terpsichorean heritage. White sergeants dash, willows are stripped and Cumberland reels at our efforts to emulate the experts we see on the demonstration video, while the owners of Hamilton House are unlikely to invite many of us to spend an evening with them, Jimmy Shand et al. But this is no introspective Scottish affair, to be indulged in by consenting clansladdies and clanslassies. French, Dutch, Swedes, Catalans, Sassenach's are all welcome, though to date only a few of the former have succumbed to the temptation.

Inevitably of course the sassenachs have turned up in numbers. That's the nature of the beasts, ever since Butcher Cumberland came to avenge the humiliation that Wallace wreaked on them at Bannockburn. To see them dance the eightsome reel together at the annual St Andrews night bash on November 30th would immediately reveal to a dispassionate observer either that not one of them has ever visited Scotland, or that they are all helplessly drunk. Both are probably true. It is a mess of randomly whirling, colliding, yelling, brainlessly grinning bodies. The *pas de basque* is particularly painful. It normally comprises one foot in the vague mid-air and the other in the groin, usually someone else's, while the arms flail the air like an out of control helicopter. It's a wonder they don't take off through the ceiling. The 'setting' is even more gruesome, rather like frogs with haemorroids dancing on hot embers.

It isn't surprising and, regrettably, it isn't just the English. Many of us are not the most fairylike of creatures either in tread or in girth, and the floor bounces and vibrates alarmingly to our rhythms - or is it our lack of them? Andrew, our wise dancemaster, has indeed wizened considerably in his brief acquaintance with us and if there were a nobel prize for patience, he would win it with ease. Jason, looking to persuade the argonauts to row against the speeding tides of the Bosphorus, could not have had it worse. But Andrew, like Jason, has had some success stories, even if he hasn't found a Golden Fleece. Although some of us are unsure as to how many pedal appendages we have at any one time, not everyone has more than one left foot. There is a Scottish Country Dancing demonstration team of which my wife, Marguerite, a consummate dancer, is a member. She flits from one-step to two-step like a true daughter of Zeus and Mnemosyne, floating elegantly in the highland mid-air, and always seeming to land on a cushion of Trossachs heather. Not all our demonstration team is so balletic. From time to time they even drag me into it. This gives the team a certain elephantine quality, but it is done reluctantly, not only because there is a shortage of male volunteers, but also because a cardiac attack is always just a figure of eight away for some of our more elderly dancers.

But we all enjoy the big caledonian events, through which various misguided Scottish exiles like me thought they could bring real culture to the Sassenachs, Franks and Gauls alike. They all turn up in their numbers, and some in kilts. Luckily no-one has yet brought any bagpipes, probably because no-one would know how to play them - not that that has ever daunted a good Scot. For St Andrews night last year, and being typically Scottish, our female members made the food for 120 people. It was a tattie hash - good wholesome Scottish autumn fare - cooked precariously in two enormous paella dishes on the top of our cooker. In order to arrive at this point, we had disrobed 40 kilos of potatoes, beheaded 10 pounds of onions, de-skinned 8 kilos of carrots and liberated the peas from ten tins. We took it in turns to rotate the dishes but a hydraulic wheel-changer would have been better. Other enthusiasts made desserts and puddings, real winter highland ones - so appropriate when the temperature was in the region of 24 degrees celsius, 75 fahrenheit. All of this was transported gingerly in the backs of cars along the road to the Village Hall where the event was to be held.

Here it was disembarked with maximum security, as if it were gold bullion, by an anxious phalanx of carriers who, with careful steps and quiet blaspheming, managed to reach the kitchen with the precious cargo. Whereupon the problem was to keep it warm, since there was no cooker there. But being British and ex-boy scouts and girl guides, we were of course prepared for such eventualities. Our small army of erstwhile land girls, air raid wardens and dad's volunteer soldiers poured the glutinous stuff into smaller receptacles and lovingly continued to stir it over camping gas stoves like a rent-a-coven of mini-witches each with its own cauldron, until it was time to dispense it to the waiting masses. To an untrained eye, it could have been the opening scene of Shakespeare's Scottish play, whose name cannot be uttered even in France.

Meanwhile, back in the hall, the Dashing White Sergeant was taking new prisoners by the minute and the Strip the Willow was creating a shrieking chaos among its new punters. The hall heaved with a prancing international bonhomie. The French appeared in large numbers to view their auld allies, the potty Scots, at their annual feast of nostalgia. Once they had been persuaded to try their hand, and their feet, the difficulty was to get them to sit down again. We resident gurus who were supposed to be demonstrating the finer points of the hop, skip or travelling jump, were overwhelmed by excited perspiring gallic masses scrambling to get stuck into the next frenetic bout of hand-slapping, toe-crunching and head-bashing.

What persuaded them to give the floor a rest was, of course, the arrival of food and drink. This method is infallible in France. As we transported the viscous liquid from kitchen to tables, noses went into the air, a strange silence ensued as the multitude homed in slowly on their own trough, like zombies to the cellar. It is true to say that there were one or two dubious glances at the offering but, hey, if this is the foie gras of the northern barbarians then at least we can give it a try.

Well, they loved it. They wolfed it down with the enthusiasm of a converted sinner, and accompanied it with copious quantities of wine and beer, the Scotch being, by this time, in very short supply. They were even gracious, or perhaps inebriated, enough to congratulate us on our merveilleuse scottish cuisine.

And so we survived. After the return to more hours of whirling, reeling and mayhem with little resemblance to dancing, the shining faces at 2 am betrayed an inner satisfaction of euphoric enjoyment and bacchanalian bliss. By the end of an exhausting and exhilarating evening we were returning home in the wee smalls with enough tattie hash to feed a small regiment and enough bottles of wine to drown a herd of camels. It wasn't that it wasn't good or appreciated - just that we had made twice as much as was required.

Homage a Burns

Our Burns nights however take on a more earnest air as befits the homage we owe to our national poet. Normally these are held between consenting Scots in the privacy of our own homes, but this year we decided to open up the pleasures of the bard to all and sundry once more in the local village hall. Many of the local French who attend these events have a smattering of English and are steadfastly prepared for the eccentricities of the britanniques in matters of national culture. But this one managed to escape them completely.

Well, look at it through the eyes of the average villager. You are a good well-brought-up, God-fearing catholic peasant. You are invited to a poetic celebration. You accept, believing it to be a major cultural event and an honour to be present. You are sitting there, contentedly enjoying the ambiance of the evening having heartily enjoyed the smoked salmon hors d'oeuvres (though all these bearded men in drag give you a somewhat worried feeling that this is perhaps not the right sort of place to bring the wife.) Then there is a hush as though something deeply poetic is about to happen. Through the door, one of the beskirted people with a fearsome black beard enters slowly through the door carrying a large tray of a quelque chose that looks like (and is) the inside of something unspeakable. He looks pleased and triumphant as if the Scots had just beat the French at Rugby (another reason to doubt the sanity of your hosts). The initial doubts are already incubating in your mind.

He is followed by yet another man in drag with a dressed-up hedgehog under his arm, squeezing the unfortunate animal and blowing into one of its orifices to the accompaniment of a tinny record-player in the distant background. Your hosts cheer loudly, as if something important really is happening. Your doubts begin to grow into misgivings about the motivation of these people and the wisdom of leaving the house this evening.

The first dragster then carefully places the tray onto a table in the middle of the room and, incredibly, begins to talk to it. 'Great chieftain of the puddin race', he starts, and continues the incantation in an unfathomably obscure accent, all the while waving his hands mysteriously over the contents of the tray, as if endeavouring to transform it into something more edible through magic. The hedgehog blower stands proudly by, though, luckily for the creature under his arm, he has stopped squeezing the life out of it and its strange orifice hangs limply by his elbow. Perhaps it is now dead!

Your hosts maintain a reverential silence during this performance. It is as if they, and you, like the thing in the dish are being mesmerized by the occult performance. The misgivings have now turned into apprehension. When will this ritual terminate? Is there any way to escape before you are sucked into the abyss? But no, things take a turn for the worse. The tartan high priest, for surely that is what he is, reaches below his skirt into his stocking top and produces a knife which he says is called dirk. He becomes more animated, plunging the knife again and again into the spewing mess and shouting loudly at it, until it oozes out onto the tray. Each time the knife falls there is a cheer from the Scottish hordes. You now know that you are in the presence of true pagan madness. But what to do? Fear holds you firmly to your seat as the performance reaches its terrifying climax. Surely to even attempt an escape would risk the wrath of the crazies in whose power you now languish. Surely the earth will now open up and Beelzebub will rise, trident in hand.

Some minutes later the high priest reaches the end of his spell, and a number of women appear from the kitchen brandishing large knives. You flinch. Perhaps your end is now nigh. The hosts, faces shining with anticipatory fervour, cheer loudly again and again. The hedgehog squeals in pain again.

What would your own emotions be at this point? What comes after fear? Terror? Panic? The urge to beat it hastily from the room? Our guests certainly showed signs of all these emotions. Jaws dropped, eyebrows raised, skin crawled and the primaeval dread of the unknown, buried under a several hundred years old veneer of gallic civilization, resurfaced. Here at last was incontrovertible proof that every Scot, indeed every person born North of la Manche, is indeed pottier than a rabid squirrel. The village hall, it seemed, had become the meeting place of a pagan cult, or at least a lunatic asylum, and if something wasn't done quickly, they might be off with the men in the white coats and certified with the rest of them. One or two of them made excuses to visit the toilet and were not seen again until they were safely in the confession box the following day.

But then something else took over. Maybe it was the courage of the damned, or the resignation of the incarcerated, or more likely the pangs of hunger as the juices of the haggis, now released from their disgusting skins, wafted over the hall. Nothing assuages peasant fear than the smell of food, even if it emanates from the insides of a Scottish sheep. Their ancestors had eaten worse during the dark days of pestilence and famine.

And so, the unsightly mess was apportioned out to each table together with the tatties and neeps, again regarded with suspicion by the villagers, since turnips are usually fodder for cattle in these parts. But by now they were now resigned to their fate. If perdition lay in store, it could wait until stomachs had been filled with whatever it was that now lay on the table and smelled so good in spite of its appearance. Sins could always be expiated in the church the following morning.

As if that were not enough, further potential torture lay ahead for the guests. Ian, (his real name is changed in case of reprisals), had prepared an evening of Scottish singing and dancing. Song-sheets, written in that strange hieroglyph, appeared on the table. The technology of modern music, amplifiers, acoustic guitars, electronic pianos, roaming microphones, which had been lurking ominously at the front of the hall, now made its malign presence felt. Jimmy Shand it wasn't, praise be - a learning experience it was. As Ian sang, the now completely submissive guests, at least those who could understand a quarter of the words, tried to understand why Donald had lost his trousers, how the gloamin' encouraged roamin', where one could find the Mull of Kintyre and the strangely intense competition between the high and the low roads. Above all they wondered why my country had suffered so badly at the hands of the Sassenachs from the South, such that someone called Charlie needed Flora to be spread on his head on his way to Skye. Resignation had given way to perplexity.

Jamie, now well into the second half of his Whisky bottle, brought his tenor voice to the execution (literally) of Bonnie Mary of Argyll and declared his undying love in the form a red, red rose, bringing a tear to the heart of every true-blooded Scotsman, a frisson of something else to the French. Some of the kilted warriors interspersed these with readings from Rabbie's poems. One of them spoke of a wee sleekit timorous beastie which, to the amazement of the guests, and the cunning smiles of the Scots, turns out to be a mouse. Talking to a mouse now! Further evidence of insanity.

But the soothing power of dance music dispels apprehension and once the same sort of bedlam experienced on the night of St Andrew had commenced, all trepidation was forgotten. The lunacy rapidly infected everyone in the hall and everything was forgotten in an orgy of chaotic bliss. These were the dances of the damned and, just for one night, might as well be enjoyed. Expiation, that spoil-sport of pleasure, could wait till the morrow.

So was my hameland poet's day celebrated in the bonnie, bonnie glens of the Conflent. It still brings a tear to my eye and a shudder to my soul.

The Conflent Tales

Chapter the Eleventh

THE MAYOR'S TALE

Being the strange story of how a beautiful Conflent village learned to love its immigrants from the northlands

The Mayor's Tale

Les Anglais, as we call them in the village - (not exactly the most original name, but that's villages in la France profonde for you) - turned up on my Mairie doorstep about 20 years ago. They said they had just bought a house down on the plain and wanted to make my acquaintance as is the custom in France (they said). Blowed if I know what custom they referred to, unless it's the traditional one of sucking up to anybody with a little bit of power, but I have to admit that my heart sank a little bit at the time. Our village has suffered a number of invasions in the past - Romans, Visigoths, Catalans, Spanish, even the Parisians - and I suppose I was thinking to myself 'Here we go again.' Not of course that I was around during the last lot, but we village folk have long race memories. And of course I was right! There are so many of the buggers here nowadays that I wonder if the hundred years war ever did end. It's a sort of second coming. I half expect to see the Black Prince buying a house next to the village Mairie.

But don't get me wrong. I have nothing personally against incomers from anywhere, as long as they behave themselves, pay their taxes and give me the respect to which I'm due. After all we're all part of Europe now, and change adds a little bit of spice. Well of course I expected the usual 'here today and gone for the next six months' sort of story, but you could have knocked me down with *la plume de ma tante* when they said they were going to be amongst us *en permanence*. They didn't look like football thugs or refugees from the stock exchange or political exiles or anything like that, and I don't expect them to be shouting 'Up Yours Pierre, Mayor of Eus' from the old village castle. They did say they had been around the world a bit - worked in foreign places like USA, Brussels and Paris. Maybe they do have some old ghosts to hide but, even now, twenty years later, I still haven't a clue why they upped sticks for our little community. But that's the British for you. Impulsive, silent, and no doubt perfidious in the end. You wouldn't find anyone down here making the reverse journey to live in Ashton-by-Wigan or Little-Grimsby-by-the-Sea (I got those names from the village Atlas and added a bit of embellishment as we French are wont to do.)

Now I'm just the humble Mayor of this tiny village in the Conflent and I don't get a huge opportunity to swan around the world, though I do keep up with what's happening in that terrible place through the TV. I even have some pretensions to a cosmopolitan culture, but we'll keep that under wraps for the time being in case it alarms the villagers. Mayoring is a full time occupation for me now that I've retired from driving the little yellow train up and down the mountain to Latour de Carol, sixty kilometres away. And that's the furthest I ever got from home. Well, it's further than most round here. I've seen sights. Driving the old engine through the gorge above St Thomas is a wonderful experience, but once you been up and down that for the three-hundredth time, the sensation tends to palls a bit. All this travelling around the world sounds just a teeny bit like the Anglais showing off their worldly sophistication at the expense of us village peasants. I have to say they do it very convincingly, but I think we peasants could teach them a thing or two about living.

Well, the *Anglais* I mentioned before (he tells me he's the immigrant in the first story – though personally I haven't read it since it's written in an alien tongue) asked me to write my story so I'd best put on my best literary hat, get out the Sunday words and fortify myself with this bottle of Cotes du Roussillon Villages they thoughtfully provided for me. It's a sight better than that rough old sump oil I make myself. So here goes. I'll let the bastards do their own translation.

The way these people talked about the first time they saw my village my chest puffed a little with pride. They're right! The first view of Eus from Route Nationale 116 *does* make for good viewing. Drivers leaving our neighbouring village of Marquixanes and crossing the railway line onto that undulating road towards Prades, can see Eus appear like a vision of paradise on the right. We in France call it a *village perché*. It has a close resemblance to a wedding cake baked by a semi-drunk chef who knew what he wanted to do but couldn't quite get the lines right – and we've had a few of those in the village I can tell you. Still have if truth were told. But no names no pack drill you understand. I might want re-election. The church plays the part of the fairy on top (and we've had a few of those too, most of them Dutch, though I shouldn't say it, because I'm not supposed to know about these things.) In clear weather, and that's what we get for much of the time in the Conflent, it presents to the eye of the passing beholder a bold, three dimensional aspect on a promontory of the near-distance hills. That description, you'll understand, is also influenced by les Anglais – they always have to make something quite simple and beautiful sound like an advertisement for Corn Flakes. But I'm not averse to their eulogising about my village. After all it is on the list of the 100 most beautiful villages in France. And the more tourists who call in for a drink at '*La Maison du Temps Libre*', as we call our Village Centre, the more profit there is for m- er the community.

Eus - rising like a wedding cake from the Garrigue. In the foreground peach blossom.

These bloody English keep ranting on about the splendours of Rocamadour, the medieval magnificence of Riquewihr and the soaring spires of Mont St Michel. Showing off if you ask me, especially when they've had a *verre* or two of our local brew. . Of course I know about them, I've seen them in my old splendours of France colour it yourself picture book. They're OK – but what they don't have is the view of the Canigou. That's our ace in the *trou* as our American friends would say. Any village which isn't only *perché*, but also has a view like that has to be the best of breed. But it's also a bit of a problem, because the village is first seen from the Route Nationale usually while driving a car. Moreover this is a road on which a good proportion of other drivers, including those apparently approaching from the opposite direction, also like to feast their eyes on the view. That tends to lead to a metaphysical impasse, those coming from one direction wishing to occupy space on both sides of the road, apparently unaware that only one car can occupy one slot in the space-time continuum. (Neat little piece of phrasing that, hein? - We French are well-known for our knowledge of the philosophy of physics, and driving that bloody train for hours on end left a lot of time for philosophising about the meaning of life.)

Anyway, that combination of factors has caused more than one car-load of people to visit the local hospital, and sometimes the mortuary, courtesy of the *sapeurs-pompiers* and the ambulance service. Perhaps they are all experiencing the Eus effect, that overwhelming gasp of surprise when confronted by a thing of beauty, but I doubt it. I don't want to say too much about the driving habits of my fellow catalans, but les anglais aren't far wrong when they describe it as a *catastrophe* preparing for a *désastre* (my italics, half them can't speak a word of our beautiful language.) Anyway, no-one should be surprised to find Catalan cars, irrespective of their final destination, at any point on the road at any time. Personally I stick to trains, where following the straight and narrow is easy, and a battered old deux chevaux which has difficulty passing a stationary pig.

The Canigou from the Maison du Temps Libre

Tiens, this wine is good – perhaps the *rosbifs* know something about it after all! Cost more than a couple of euros I'll guess. Not used to the expensive stuff. So here's to international harmony. Anyway, as I was saying, when I so rudely interrupted myself, most casual visitors enter my village *en voiture*, crossing the river Têt by the single narrow bridge below the village. They immediately know that they are entering somewhere special, paradise perhaps or the parish of heavenly delights or simply the most beautiful village on God's earth. They thread their way round the hairpins to the top. Those ascending have difficulty in avoiding those descending, partly because the road is quite narrow – we're a bit cramped for space here - and partly because some of them don't, for very good reasons, want to drive too close to the edge. Very few of our visitors know the real width of their cars. When they reach the top they park the car, always providing that any slots remain in *le parking*. But it doesn't matter really whether they are there or not. If there aren't any they park it anyway, usually in the most inconvenient place they can find. I wouldn't admit it to those foreigners but my fellow Frenchmen are not the most considerate of people when it comes to following the rules.

Anyway, whoever they are, they have a brief wonder at the spectacular view of the valley of Prades and the breathtaking panorama of the Canigou from the terrace of the *Maison du Temps Libre*, our village hall.

I can't remember why we called it that – I seem to have very little free time myself. Anyway, as I was saying, they then amble aimlessly along the narrow *rue* towards the church at the highest point of the village. Funny how everyone does that. The local *curé* says it's because they are seeking God, but somehow I have my doubts – there *is* a convenient shop selling drinks up there as well. They will climb with increasingly aching limbs - I know, I still find it a trudge at the best of times even after a couple of stiff ones - up the cobbled slope and the time-worn stone *escalier* to the church entrance.

This upper church (we have a lower one, also dedicated to the same Saint Vincent, and that's only been around for 600 years longer) has been formally closed, though not deconsecrated, for many a long year and it's only used for special services at Christmas, Easter and the feast day of our village patron saint. Not many visitors risk life and limb climbing the stairs to the top of the tower - for one thing the wood is inhabited by some thousands of creatures for whom wood is a daily bread, and for another, the stones at the top have a disturbing tendency to move when looked at in a certain way. To be honest, it's a little bit of an imposition on the villagers, who have to pay their whack towards its restoration. After all it was built more than 360 years ago. But none of us, even the honest, and dishonest, doubters and the straightforward atheists, would ever begrudge conserving this little piece of their history.

But, if the great studded wooden church door is open, the grock – er welcome visitors, will go inside and peer at the rude simplicity of its seating arrangements, a few wooden forms spread across the aisle. What a contrast these are to the ornate ostentation of the baroque *retable.* Good word that and you'll find a few *bons mots* in this piece! – the wine helps - they tell me it's called an altarpiece in English. It dominates the front wall – it *is* the front wall. Being a Catalan born and bred, I can't help feeling very *fier* of these *retables.* Almost every church in the area has one, and there was a good living to be had for itinerant seventeenth century baroque altar designers with a dash of careful creativity. And we're *exceptionablement* proud of ours. The curé tells me that it was carved by the same Sunyer brothers who did the big one in Prades. And there's another thing about our church. The altar, unusually, is at the west end of the apse, so that people pray with their backs to the East. That's quite a status symbol in religious terms. We haven't told the pope about it yet.

The Retable in Eus Church

nyhow, where was I? Merde, this wine is good! Did I tell you I made it myself?. Oh yes *l'eglise*, the church as those d...d English call it! And the welcome visitors. Well, if they haven't been warned in advance, they will meet one of my most interesting village characters inside. Jean-Paul is an enthusiast. What he doesn't know about every stone of the church, its history, geography, artefacts and what has happened to them in the last 400 years can be written on the nail of his little finger. What he does know takes several hours to relate. Those benigh- er nice English told me about a poem about an ancient mariner with a bony hand who stoppethed (is that really an English word?) the arriving guests at a wedding. Apparently he managed a 1 in 3 success rate. Jean-Paul would not be satisfied with less than 98% and his hand is considerably less bony.

Quand'même, as the casual visitors, - for after all, this is how most callers into the Eus church would describe their original intention - gradually adjust their corneal muscles from the brilliant sunshine which forever seems to shine on our village (it is my proud boast that we are *le village le plus ensoleille en France* – fact!) to the relative gloom of the interior, they are swept into a rapidly expanding sea of bewildered faces seemingly waiting for something big to happen – a new miracle perhaps or, more hopefully, water turning into free wine, or indeed simple parole.

Just another sip and I'll continue. I never knew that my own wine tasted so good. Now what was I saying? Oh yes, Jean-Paul. Well, when he invites these peas... er guests to 'come in and sit down' one metre inside the portal it's not so much a word of welcome as an order. It takes a strong and improbably impolite personality to refuse it. Those captives already entrapped nod knowingly and sympathetically to each newcomer into the fold. When he considers that he has a large enough audience, at least 15 and often more, Jean Paul describes, in fast and furious catalan-accented french, the background, composition and purpose of every statue, every item on the *'retable'*, every picture and every small chapel in the building. As the word count mounts rapidly into a fat thesaurus, the prisoners sit in the bum-numbing pews in which generations of Yllicians have worshipped; they experience the stations of the cross, as did our forebears; they are led on a visual and oral tour of the building and they are amazed at the richness of its treasures; they are invited to ring the angelus bells and they rejoice with the angels; they are enjoined to examine the nooks and crannies and they obey.

It is a veritable tour de force - the short version lasts about one hour and a half and woe betide anyone who tries to slink off. Jean-Paul has a knack of inserting himself between his detainees and the exit. And it takes place 3 or 4 times a day in the season. What is more it is interesting – even those who have experienced a good lunch manage to stay awake (they'd better!), and far more so than most of the sermons delivered in the same place on special occasions. Jean-Paul's deep and knowledgeable enthusiasm for everything within his domain is infectious. An observer counting the visitors in and counting them out again would see them arrive with an air of indifference and leave, eyes staring wildly, in a confused daze - from the wonder that anyone could remember such a wealth of detail, from the experience of concentrating hard on the speed and timbre of the words, from their re-emergence from the gloom into the brightness of a world now shining upon the recently acquired knowledge churning inside their heads. Many a planned meeting has been delayed and many a meal uneaten - even here in la France profonde. Thanks to Jean-Paul, the religion of the soul has triumphed over the religion of the flesh.

My word this wine gets better with every sip. Strange how the bottle has suddenly emptied itself. I must have spilled some while concentrating. Never mind there's another one that Dutch couple gave me last week. So what was I saying? Ah yes the Sermon on the Mount. Yes well, that's usually it for the tourists. Eager to get on to the next sight in the Michelin Green guide and having been detained rather longer in our village than they had planned, they will retrace their steps, perhaps strolling through the tunnel beneath the church, back to the car park from where they will drive back down the winding road to face the perils of the highway. But what treasures they have missed! In my opinion, to obtain the best return on his investment of time, any visitor to our village should enter it from its lowest point and walk upwards, ever upwards, through the narrow, steep, stone-cobbled *'carrers'* or alleys, winding here and there in random disarray. And here's where I'm going to get out the official village brochure. (Hey, this new bottle's not bad either)

He, or she, would wander past flower-bedecked, tight-packed cottages renovated in all styles and shapes, pass underneath grandiose arches and through neat and tiny squares, redolent with bougainvillaea and passion fruit. He might go into the old village school-house, now a museum of village antiquity, displaying the hopes, beliefs, fashions, activities, artefacts and occupations of villagers from long ago. Each house in the village seems to achieve the seemingly impossible dream of having a view over the valley toward the raw majesty of the Canigou mountain, snow-covered for nine months of the year and rising like a massive eagle's wing 9000 feet into the stratosphere. Those who have not made that journey leave behind the grieving unexplored soul of a community like no other community on earth. If I wax lyrical about the beauty of my village, forgive me. It's also the essence of my own soul and I am in perfect love and harmony with it.

I sometimes feel sorry for the pagans of the North. They are not Catholics, so how could they expect to understand our customs and *patrimoine*?. I think they once told me they were nothing more than honest but hopeful doubters. I ask you, what's that supposed to mean? These Brits don't seem to be able to make their minds up about anything of importance. Maybe it also explains their attitude to Europe. But many of them *are* members of the celebrated Chorale of Eus and they *do* regularly sing mass with the rest of the Choir in spite of their lack of any spiritual values. And we don't make many concessions to the *étrangers* in our midst when we celebrate mass in our catalan-accented, breakneck French. They don't seem to mind. For them it may be the honest act of a doubtable God – whatever that means , seems this wine is stronger than I thought..

Just a few more facts and figures about my village to bore you for completeness and boredom. The commune of Eus comprises another 360 souls - I use the phrase advisedly in honour of both our churches of St Vincent, one at the lowest point of the village dating back to the 10th century, and the other, as I said, a baroque glory built in the grounds of a long-destroyed hill-top castle to celebrate the glories of the counter-reformation in the 17th century. The Valhalla half of these souls looks down with haughty disdain from the pristine white tiers of the village itself onto the lesser mortals, mostly peach farmers, who live on the plain by the river below. *Les anglais*, the immigrants as they call themselves, though by no means peach farmers themselves, also live on the plain. They were the first of a procession of permanent invaders, Dutch, English, Scottish and Welsh (why do these British make such distinctions - the 'Royaume Unie' doesn't seem to me to match up to its last word any more than Grande Bretagne lives up to its first).

I mentioned that we have about 360 inhabitants (but they're not sharing *this* wine with me – it's too good for them). But despite its smallness, Eus is also something of a cultural centre for the whole valley. It attracts the arty-farty from miles around. At various points of the week one can see the aesthetically-inclined paint, the energetically-prone performing miracles of movement in order to keep fit (and indeed 'prone' is *le mot juste* at its completion), the musically-disposed sing (well, almost) and the intellectually-bent receive courses on the art of the baroque or 17th century Catalan literature and other such esoterica. Jeanne, our village culture vulture, sees to all that nonsense, because she thinks she's a superior intellectual – bit like the Brits really. Just read her tale below. The rest of us know differently. But in our little village hall, locals and *étrangers* alike paint their designs on every type of surface under the sun - paper, glass, plastic, concrete, leather, stone, fabric, human skin I wouldn't doubt - nothing and no-one is safe from the predatory painters of Eus. All of this is under the ever-watchful eye of the resident expert, and all is financial fodder for the frequent *kermesses* from which innocent tourists take the products far and wide across Europe. It amuses me that, throughout the continent, in the parlour of a German Bauhaus, on the dressing table of a British semi or on the shelf of a Swedish Sauna, there are glass bottles or pieces of brightly coloured stone or leather whatnots painted by the matrons of Eus. It is a sobering thought (although not just yet) and one which gives me much pride.

Like I said before I took this last swig, most of these activities take place in the *maison du temps libre*. Here we also teach people to dance the *Sardane*, the local Catalan folk ballet, seemingly simple to perform by watching, but in practice fiendishly difficult to do well. Even some of the British contingent takes part. I had been told that they were shy and reserved, watchers and admirers rather than doers and activists. Someone must have got this wrong. I have to say that I watch with wonder as the Dutch and English prance and high-step their way round our national dance. Of course they could not possibly perform all the steps perfectly, only we Catalans can do that, and it involves careful counting to more than ten. But the delicacy of movement displayed by these barbarians from the North, even those who are built more for the rugby scrum than the dance floor, sometimes astounds me.

People celebrate the sardane

When the invasion started, we feared for our culture, our patrimoine and some of us for our lives. We frequently see on television the antics the British and the Dutch get up to at football matches. But I have to say that most of them, much to my surprise, do play a full part in village life. Our villagers are themselves a mixture of indigenous Catalan locals and immigrants from other parts of France. Some of them even come from Paris, but we'll draw a discreet veil over that – they don't usually admit to it after a couple of weeks here. But I'm very proud of my *étrangers,* and not only because they pass me a bottle of this wonderful red stuff every now and then (hola - it looks like this one's got away again – now where's that 2006 vintage that new Welshman gave me last week?) These *Britanniques* who have settled here have come to know many of the other villagers quite well - at least as well as we allowed them to - and the great majority of my villagers are wonderful hosts. Much to their, and I suspect our, surprise, they have been welcomed unconditionally into the village, adopted as neighbours. They seem to be so surprised when we share our produce without asking anything in return and at how little resentment there is at the invasion of so many étrangers in our midst. But that's our way in the countryside. What has helped is that they have tried hard to integrate into their new community. They learn with us on class days, sell their wares with us on *kermesse* days, empty their attics with us on *vide-grenier* days, feast with us on feast days and sing with us on choir days. World travellers they may have been, but for its new inhabitants Eus is the epicentre of the universe. They have even influenced some of the natives, who are now straying beyond village boundaries to other far-flung places such as Prades (4 kms), Ille-sur-Tet (10 kms) and even to the outer galactic city of Perpignan (40 kms). Having driven that yellow job up and down the mountain for 40 years I too like to think of myself as a world traveller.

Eus in Music

We're particularly proud of our musical heritage in Eus (I have to modestly admit to having an acceptable bass voice - some say the best in the choir – well my wife does anyway!). Now I know that our *chef de choeur* has written about the choir but I just want to get my two centimes-worth as well. For my euros we're the best in the valley, perhaps in the whole department. And that's in no small part due to the *étrangers*, who seem to rule each part of the choir with an iron tongue. Sometimes its embarrassing to be corrected by silver-tongued pagans from our old enemy but even I can hear that the singing standard in general has gone up since they arrived.

That doesn't of course go for their pronunciation. In general they massacre the French language in a barely acceptable manner, and half of them don't understand a word they are singing. But we rub it in hard when it comes to singing in Catalan. That's our speciality. You should hear their efforts to pronounce some of the most simple phrases! And I have to admit we are very hard on them. We pounce upon each mispronunciation as if it were a capital offence. We turn their thoughts and mouths toward the straight and narrow of linguistic purity. But it works and I am often impressed by the rapidity with which some of our non-natives learn. I have to say, reluctantly, that, in the end, some of them murder the Catalan better than the natives, but then not everyone speaks the language round here.

The *etrangers* seem to find hundreds more opportunities to exercise their vocal chords than we do. And I can understand completely the circumstances in which they do it. (That last mouthful made me feel like breaking into song as I write these words.) Many are the times when I and some of my fellow villagers have been invited to a party thrown by *les britanniques* where everyone seems to end up singing, or rather butchering, since the copious quantities of wine seem to diminish the quality of the voices, popular folk songs from all parts of Europe. I understand they call it singing for your supper, but I never heard of such a tradition in Catalonia. Some of these same people seem to attend such parties as often as four times a week. The village resounds with music. I personally don't know how they can survive the assault on both their vocal chords and their inner digestive processes simultaneously.

The other way we have a silent laugh at the britanniques is the French welcome. You can see that the poor saps, especially the males, are uncomfortable when it comes to the *petits bisous*. The barely concealed look of terror on the faces of some of the men as our ladies approach with osculatory intent tells its own story. The first anglais immigrant was particularly reticent, especially with my wife, and to her shame she took full advantage of the poor man's hesitation. It's OK now of course. She relented from her silent laughter, and offered the necessary expiation, but the poor man was in a state of embarrassed indecision for weeks. Should he, shouldn't he - will she, won't she - what the hell is happening? Do I want to be here. We had a good laugh about that I can tell you. His wife, on the other hand, familiarised herself as if she were born to it. Perhaps she has some fiery French blood in her veins from long ago. At the drop of a beret she will wade into a crowd of people, lips in permanent purse, osculating like Rudolph Valentino on Speed. It is an education to see and an exercise in adaptive learning.

Mind you, singing is not our only musical accomplishment. Our yllician (for so we inhabitants of Eus call ourselves, though many don't know why) musical culture would not be complete without an instrumental group, though culture would be perhaps too strong a word to use for the Band'Eus. Two saxophones, a flute, an accordion, piano, 2 drummers and various zealous percussionists, of which I admit to having been one, provided music to dance to. Our Great Leader in this case was also Dutch. Sadly we fell out with our band leader and he with us. But that hasn't stopped the tradition. In its place, like a phoenix rising from the ashes, rose another village band, calling itself the 'Brigade Internationale'. I ask you! What a name for a dance band – they must be a bunch of aging communists. And of course who is the leader of that group of aging rockers but the immigrant anglais on the keyboard? With a gallois belting the bejasus out of the drums, a Dutch saxophonist from the old lot trying to mix the notes in the right combination, a French bass guitar providing a dubious rhythm and another English lead guitar eager to recreate 1960s triumphs in a place which never heard them in the original anyway, it provides a worthy successor. And I have to say though that, even without me to guide them, they jazz up the music like the other lot never did. On fête days both the choir and the band are in continual demand and continuous motion. And so are the dancers - they circulate vertiginously to the waltz, trot sedately to the fox-trot and step quickly to the quickstep. Sometimes they do all three at once when the band hasn't quite got it right. But the real chaos occurs when they do their rock sessions. The noise! The frenetic behaviour of the boppers, boogying their hearts out, and their health away like demented orang-outangs. It's all too much for a village with traditions.

By contrast, the Eus 'Thé Dances' are always well-attended, being known throughout the region as havens of opportunity - for perfection in dancing of course, other purposes being beyond the scope of my remit.

They are outwardly staid affairs on the afternoon of first Sunday in the month. The average age of the attendee is well in advance of 60 and the twist, the rock, the locomotion and the jive, those antiquated expressions of yesteryear's more energetic individualism, now passé and dated, are not abundantly conspicuous at these happy occasions. Rather the more stately and venerable dances of the Paris Lyceum yesteryesteryear, no doubt daring in their time - the veleta, the St Bernard Waltz , the tango, the cha-cha - rule the brain, heart and floor. Our most lively rhythms are South, rather than North, American in origin and this reflects my region's Spanish ancestry and its proximity to that country.

It has come to my attention that our *thé danses* are not popular with the *etrangers*. I guess they may think themselves too highly sophisticated and worldly-wise for the simple pleasures of us villagers. It *is* true that there is an element of time slippage. In embracing the refinement of a past age I suppose that we are showing two fingers, British-style, to the phreneticism of a changing world. But there is some evidence that they are maturing. One or two of them turned up last time. I'm confident we shall have them all eventually, and with it the stability they so desperately seek. Living in the timelessness of the Conflent can inflict fatal damage on long-held preconceptions.

Just one more slurp before I put this to bed for the night. Writing this piece seems to have unlocked the verbal diarrhoea I used to have when eating all those escargots.

Famous Yllicians

Back again – it's morning and time to open another bottle. What was I saying – oh yes, my village. Folklore has it that it has been graced by famous names in the past. Before my time the epiglottal Belgian singer, Jacques Brel, owned a house here, though no-one can ever remember seeing him visit it, or even which dwelling-places it was! More debatably, the famous and wonderful Edith Piaf, queen of the vibrating throat and a legend in her own time, is said to have bought one of our village dwelling-places. I can neither confirm nor deny that this is so - after all why should I? But between you and me, this story should be dedicated to

Apocrypha - it is probably true much in the same way that the number of beds Napoleon is reputed to have slept in would have kept him dormant for twice his lifetime.

Our present claim to stardom by association (apart from the *etrangers* of course) is that Ursula, the widow of Boris Vian lives here. Boris who? I hear you say, and you would be right to do so. But if you had lived in Paris during the late 1940s and early 50s, you may have vaguely heard of the poet, author of '*L'écume des jours*', and jazz trumpeter at a time when jazz was de rigueur in France. We, out in the agricultural sticks certainly hadn't. Any way, I'm told that Boris was the acknowledged leader of the so-called Saint Germain set, *bon viveurs* and *philosophes* who frequented the cafes and nightlife near to the Boulevard Saint Germain à *l'époque*. Names we learned about in school and promptly forgot, Jean-Paul Sartre, Simone de Beauvoir et al who, when they were not existentialising about the real meaning of life, became the bosom *copains* of our Boris. As it happens he died of his excesses in 1959.

I mention this because Ursula ran the Boris Vian foundation. Every August it organises concerts in the village for the tourists and the villagers. Most of them have a Catalan flavour and include some of the best guitarists and dancers in the region - but there is also Jazz and every 2 years there is a blockbuster. I can take or leave jazz - for me it isn't very French - but les anglais go quite potty about this. They told me that they were great fans of the music of a guy called Jacques Loussier, who ran a trio some years ago. Now I know that at least two of my fellow scribes have mentioned this but it only means something when the Mayor writes it. And that's me. Anyway they reckoned it would cost 100 euros and more to hear the trio play in Paris, New York or London. That's almost a month's takings at the community centre bar, so they *must* be famous. So when the beggers appeared to play Bach at a Boris Vian Foundation concert in our village hall - for 5 euros - I swallowed my pride and went along too, and I have to say that they were indeed good. Maybe not the style of Aznavour or the panache of Michel Legrand or the enthusiasm of Johnny Halliday, but quite good in an odd sort of way. I certainly wouldn't have paid 100 euros even if I could have afforded it (and between you and me I didn't pay the 5, me being the mayor and all) but that's a matter of taste I suppose. Sadly Ursula died a couple of years ago, but her name, and the festival lives on.

Village Characters

All villages have their special characters. They would not be villages without them. And mine is no exception. Now I wouldn't normally get to indulge in gossip about my flock of without a few sips of this wonderful Chateaux Legrand, but its true that Eus has a veritable cornucopia of characters. According to the Gallois who lives at the bottom of the village it's a sort of

French 'Under Milk Wood' without the intrigue, so I'll take his word for it without actually knowing what the hell he's prattling on about. Personally I think he's been at the meths, or talking to the sheep as I understand most Welsh people do – and worse. It's not that we think he's a bit potty but he does burble on about some characters called Organ-Morgan, Mrs Ogden Pritchard, Captain Cat and says that he can recognise them in the village as Catalan counterparts. I think that he's a bit weird because I know for fact that there's no-one with those names within a hundred kilometres of here.

So I'm going to take one more little snifter (I tell you, this 2003 Dom Brial the Swedes gave me last week is something special) and tell you about my characters. It would be wrong to say that we laugh at them as if they were village idiots. Rather we laugh with them because they are loveable and generous and they add colour and interest and vibrancy and pleasure. I will of course change the names to protect the innocent. There is Nicole, a lady who walks 3 times a day to the *supermarche* in Prades and back with her dog for no other reason than that it is something to do. She is outwardly pleasant and lucid and charming and articulate. This being the deep south, some of our more superstitious villagers think that she'a sorciere, and want the old ducking stool brought out of hibernation. Personally I consign all that nonsense to the annals of history, probably because I don't want to make the national press as the Mayor who murdered a witch. I do sometimes wonder though if she is a philosopher *manqué* who has discovered a secret which has so far escaped the rest of us. Then there is Jacques, a farmer of great age, who takes all younger people under his tutelage, especially if they are *étrangers.* Some believe him to be centuries old and some say he is actually quite young. He follows his 4 cows from pasture to pasture for most of the day but when he is not doing this he is trying to make good peasants of the britanniques, a project doomed to failure if you ask me. He dispenses knowledge and opinion on all subjects rural without obligation, without rancour and without being asked to. For him the britanniques are the ignorant of the ignorant, to be pitied for their dangerous lack of survival skills in this awful pastoral paradise, and he has mounted a one-man campaign to share his ancient wisdom with them. To soften them up he showers them with presents from the bounty of his farm - peaches, nectarines, vegetables, flowers, always leaving before they can mutter a thank-you . He plans their gardens for them us according to the phases of the moon, as we all do in these parts. The idiots among them laugh and sneer at what they see as piece of pagan baloney, but we know what works and what doesn't and who's ignorant and who isn't. There is a moontime to plant onions and beans (the waxing) and another to plant things which grow downwards into the earth (waning time). There is a unique moontime to harvest certain vegetables and fruits to obtain maximum freshness and preserving quality. Even the weather is affected by the moon. To their over-conditioned urban minds, overwhelmed as they are by the arrogance of scientific certainty, this might sound ingenuous, a load of old bobbins, but most of them come to realise that, in our ancient minds, there lies a vast pool of arcane knowledge. Somehow, on the journey to their so-called enlightenment, they have lost the art of wonder, the harmony with nature and the power that influences inner thoughts and feelings. Far be it from me to suggest that it's them that are the loonies, but........

In French village life there are also some customs that exercise the brains, if that is what they can be called, of the etrangers. For example, the anglais that calls himself the immigrant moved into a farmhouse on the plain below the village. This was part of a farm which was split between two brothers, Jean and Gilles, on the death of their father. Jean received the farmhouse and Gilles the farm buildings and the meadow on which to feed his cows in winter. Since that day in 1963, the two brothers never addressed one word to each other. So Jean sold his half of the deal to our anglais. Well of course I could have told him. It was like a red rag to a bull. It compounded the feud. Gilles son, Gilles himself having passed away, implacably refuses to speak to the new owners and does his best to make their life difficult. He has even put up a sign on his gate about Jeanne d-Arc being burnt by the English in 1431, hoping that that would provoke some anger. I'm told that the Anglais are quite proud of it, always insisting that their visitors have a photograph taken next to the sign. All attempts at reconciliation are met by a centuries old tradition in these parts of hostility to anything new or different, though time and what the anglais calls his natural charm – must say I haven't noticed it - have reduced the standoff to an uneasy peace. So what's new? Why do the brits seems to think it strange that a catalan farmer with a millennium of the tradition of fighting with his neighbours and his mind still in the hundred years war, should continue to do what comes naturally? That sort of thing is commonplace? Similar stories can be multiplied throughout rural France – just read Jean de Florette and Manon des Sources. They are part of every village's folklore – and ours is no exception.

 I'm just debating with myself whether or not to open this bottle of Tautavel the new Scots brought today. It's not really local and – oh what the hell – the Dom Brial seems to have disappeared. Someone must have moved it. Anyway, as I meant to say, not all villagers are like Gilles. Some of them have moved at least into the 19th Century, when Napoleon the 3rd was quite fond of the English. And hardship often changes attitudes. Most of the peach farmers now speak to each other, some of them without gritting their teeth, and they even help each other out in times of emergency. But they can too become extremely defensive about the limits of their land. One well-known and well-loved farmer who sits on my *conseil municipal*, put a plank across the ditch at the edge of his field to enable him to clear it better. Strange how a simple plank can inflame passions. The next week he received a letter from the solicitor of the neighbouring *agriculteur*, not so well-loved in the village, demanding that he remove the plank which now abutted onto his land. Strangely enough, the number of planks seems to have multiplied .....

Village Feasting

I can confidently say, especially after a couple of swigs of the Muscat de Rivesaltes donated by the Danish people who think they were trying to buy favour, that we eat very well in my village. There are many feast days but I intend to describe only two and those only briefly. These are the feast of the *boles de picolat* and the Day of the Giant Paella, two of the major village fêtes. *Boles de Picolat* are a local Catalan winter delicacy of meat balls cooked with herbs and spices and served in a thick meat sauce. They are served together with large white haricot beans as an accompaniment, with all that that entails for days afterwards. Giant paellas are - well, giant paellas. The former, a winter warmer, is served on the village Saints day, St Vincent, which occurs on the 22nd January every year, and it is as well to put one's name down on the list early, for it's epicurean pleasures are in great demand throughout the region. After the incomparable Eus Chorale, of which you will recall I am a member, has done its euphonious bit in the mass at a freezing church, we get first shot at the feast. This commences with the inevitable aperitifs of Muscat de Rivesaltes, available in quantities which would quickly exhaust the capacity of a hippopotamus. When everyone has found a seat at one of the four trestle tables each stretching the length of the hall, a process which for some reason or other seems to take at least an hour and to be best accomplished amid a deafening buzz of chatter, the serious business of eating begins.

The first indication of this is the appearance of plates loaded with cooked meats - *tête de veau*, at which the *etrangers* seem to shudder. God knows why. I never did understand this abhorrence of perfectly good brains. Same goes for blood since a delicious *boudin noir* also finds its way onto the plate with *langue de veau* and *jambon cru.* Of course the villagers plunge into this with relish and only the plates on the britannique table remain mostly untouched. Ungrateful buggers. They might as well not have come at all. They do however eat the lettuce served with it. Bunch of bloody rabbits if you ask me. Anyway, to continue the story with a sip of this good domaine amiel, one could be forgiven for believing that this is the main course so much have the punters put away. However, then comes the *pièce de resistance* supervised by Michèle, my wonderful wife. First, the bowls of *haricots blancs* are spaced at judicious intervals on the tables. Then Michèle, together with several helpers, britanniques included, brings out the enormous bowls containing the meat balls and, to deafening cheers, tours the tables ladling large quantities of the bovine and porcine lumps onto each plate. By the time she has reached the last recipient it is time to start over again, and other unpaid, unsung but much-loved servants recommence the *tour des tables*. This rondelay goes on until everyone is replete to bursting and can eat no more. Naturally, red and rosé wine are free-flowing, just like this bottle of red I just opened

From time to time during this pandemonium, the congregation, led by Our Great Choirleader, will burst, not quite spontaneously but certainly very willingly, into song. There is then a short rest to clear some stomach space, during which more songs are cheerfully crucified, before the next culinary assault. This is the cheese course, a further glorious opportunity to tank up on a selection of cholesterol-filled delights. More singing ensues though of dubious quality, since the wine, and the large quantities of food already consumed, have already had a deleterious effect on the vocal chords. More space having been created by this hiatus, another seasonal delicacy of the region, the *'galette des rois'*, a sort of sweetish shortcake containing a small item of pottery called a *feve* which one has to be careful not to swallow, makes its triumphant appearance. He or she who receives the piece with the pottery becomes king or queen of the meal and is condemned to wear a silly golden crown for the rest of the day, a dubious privilege but one accepted graciously, largely as a result of a generous intake of wine. He, or she, who swallows the feve spends an uncomfortable night while it works its way through the various tubes and pipes until it miraculously reappears the following day, too late, alas, to wear the crown. The afternoon passes noisily into evening when more individual, group and congregational singing transforms strained bonhomie into undying love.

It is perhaps barely worth mentioning at this point that four of the male *britanniques* of the choir combine eagerly in this concert with a spirited rendering in English of the two gendarmes (obviously their sodden brains affect their counting skills) from the famous Offenbach operetta, *Geneviève de Brabant*. This well-known song is ritually murdered while wearing large plastic, British-style policemen's helmets and with truncheons held in various states of aloft.

Normally, this brings the house down. Although the punters haven't understood a single word that was sung, the slapstick is pure Benny Hill, and the applause is generous – a grievous mistake since, as an encore, they perform an agonising hands-on-shoulder number called Side by Side followed by an excruciating rendering of that well-known French chanson, 'Old Father Thames'. Not to be outdone (why do these events always turn into a competition?) individual, and quite inebriated, French members of the chorale make their own atonal contributions and the night passes into a horror version of Dante's Inferno. Several people now hurriedly leave the feast either because they are still moderately sober or because the beans are having their effect.

And so it is with the Day of the Giant Paella, normally consumed on the *Fête de St Jean* in June. It is a continuing story of gluttony and carousal following a similar pattern to the boles de picolat, but with one addition. The *Fête de St Jean* is a longest day midsummer madness festival dating back to pagan times, and we all know what those people got up to when they had a skinful. As dusk falls, a huge bonfire is lit over which the young, and not so young, men of the village are expected to jump. He who does not make this epic leap misses out on the chances of pulling the birds - one uses the vernacular because this is a vernacular festival - for the rest of the year. That is, it is a fertility rite of passage. The fire is kept deliberately low in case the result of jumping over it would be the equivalent of not having done so. Burning ardour has its physical limitations. The age of the hopeful jumpers varies from 6 to 86, thus demonstrating the charming naivety of the child, the buoyant expectation of the adolescent, the misplaced optimism of the middle-aged and the sheer desperation of the wrinklies. Scorched trousers can be found the following day in almost every Conflent village. In another manifestation of psychotic lunacy, there is a tradition which requires young men to run down the Canigou mountain in the pitch dark bearing flaming torches. While it is a spectacular way of passing the time, the danger it poses is all too apparent in the local hospital in the early hours of the morning.

These are just two of the many days that the inhabitants of my village spend in celebrating their great luck in living in such a plentiful place. I too am fortunate in that I can serve them, and also receive so many presents of this wonderful wine I am now drinking. I can't claim that it is unique in all France but if anyone has a better experience, I'd be interested to hear it.

A game of Petanque

I'm being told to bring this tale to an end. Don't know why. I've really only just begun. There's so much more to say, but the *britannique* reckons that there are limits to a reader's patience, and, after all he bought me a case of fine *Cotes du Roussillon Villages* to write it. He who pays the piper and all that. As a last throw, I can't help telling you about one other activity we men get up to every summer. No french village would be complete without the wherewithal to play the game of *petanque* - boules as the Brits erroneously call it. Situated a few metres below the *Maison du Temps Libre* is a square of gravel-covered waste-land optimistically called a boulodrome. It is here that the men of the village congregate in summer at around 10 pm to scatter their balls of iron until well into the new day. And, much to their chagrin, it is not only men who turn up at these occasions. It has been known to harbour more than 4 simultaneous games of gesticulating, vociferating, altercating mixed members of humanity within its confines. Pétanque players are not born with innate qualities of sportsmanship and fair play. In its morality, it is to the French what croquet is to the English - superficially genteel but below the surface a hotbed of intrigue, rule manipulation and jealously protected territories. Many of the women who play the game tend to roll the ball in the manner of English bowls. This is considered to be unsporting and ungentlemanly by the men, but it is tolerated because - well, because they are women. It certainly leads to more accuracy more of the time, and causes some occasional embarrassment to the male ego when there is a female victory.

The Eus boulodrome also has some other special characteristics. It slopes and therefore requires special techniques and knowledge to play it. I'm told that, in the North of England, there are bowling greens that are deliberately not flat – they have a 'crown' in the middle to confuse the southerners and foreigners. Well, our boulodrome is a little like that. Local knowledge counts for all, the exact number of metres to lance the boule to the left or the right so that it comes to rest gently by the *cochonet* being a well-kept secret uncovered only after a long and painful apprenticeship. The wife of Eus is one of the few women who do not roll the ball. She has a perfect pétanque delivery action which launches the ball some metres into the air and strikes terror into partners and opponents alike. She is a very good '*pointeuse*', usually getting at least 2 of her 3 balls close to the *little pig,* and even the local French players swallow their pride and enrol her on their team. Good *pointeurs* are difficult to find. Most red-blooded male *pétanquistes* like to be *tireurs*, the players who viciously attack the opponent's ball and knock it out of play with a well-aimed blow. We're very good at that. I myself am one of the best. The britanniques thought they had developed a technique fpr minimising the success of our aerial bombardments by throwing the cochonet far into the distance. That's cheating. In fact anything that prevents we locals from winning is cheating – one of the unwritten rules of the Eus boulodrome. So we declared a local rule (again unwritten) that 10 metres is the longest possible end. Well, it's our pitch and there is very little the others can do.

But it seems that the *étrangers* have the gift of adapting to new sports, a kind of bent for ex-patriate games. Especially, it seems, those who played a lot of cricket. I don't know what it is about these people from the Northern islands. Can't they see that losing at our national game is part of the price they have to pay for letting them live among us? But no, they just have to win. Here's just an example of how they do it. This haunts my memory like an unwanted phantom. It occurred while the score was level at 12 each. We were playing a team of *Britanniques* and superbly confident of winning at last. With our penultimate ball, we had sneakily succeeded in moving the *cochonet* on towards the very limit of the boulodrome some 22 yards away and our winning ball was snuggling up close. The ten metre rule seemed to have been quietly forgotten in the excitement of finally putting one over those smug bastards. They had one ball left. The distance was at the limit of the possible and, since they were at the limit of desperation they could only bomb, And weren't we the champions at such macho techniques? We were told that their last man was well-known in UK cricket circles for his ability to demolish opposition teams with donkey droppers onto the top of the wicket, whatever that means. Load of old *merde* that.

Anyway he stepped up to the mark wearing that smug-bugger smile that all the *etrangers* can put on when confronted with an impossible task. He looked upwards as if was praying to the heavens for inspiration or intervention - rain, lightning, flood, death - anything. We

French knew that this was all show. We already had the game won and were looking forward to making them buy the drinks for a change. Still wearing his Gioconda Smile, he launched his boule into the stratosphere, and this where I get lyrical. Upwards it soared, defying the laws of gravity with an aerodynamic perfection. Mouths agape, both adversaries and supporters watched its awesome trajectory. At what seemed to be 2000 feet, but in reality was probably not more than 20, it ran out of upward mobility and commenced its terrible plunge. Like the latest blueprint for a heat-seeking missile, it homed in on the poor *cochonet*. I swear that we all saw it tremble in its helplessness. Then, with an impact that was massive and mighty, the unstoppable force met the immovable object, shattering the poor wooden pig into a thousand tiny pieces and scattering them to all parts of the village. There was a pregnant silence while the awful truth dawned. That one individual shot will live in the history of the village and be recorded for generations into the 30th century, and it was thrown by a bloody Englishman. The supercilious sod acknowledged the miracle and the applause with the slight movement of the hand as if this was an everyday occurrence.

That's just what we most admire, and hate, about the britanniques. They never know when they are beaten . What's more, they seem to take over everything – the choir the committees, the *petanque*, There's even one of them on that bastion of Frenchness, the conseil municipal. It's getting to be like a virus. At least they can't take over my job – that's the law in France!

I have tried to present the annual round of life in our village through its activities and its people. Of course much more happens here than I have space to describe, and much more happens than we have knowledge of. Villages have their secrets. But, like most French villages, it waltzes to the rhythm of the seasons and carries its inhabitants along with the dance. It is a good life and one in which we participate to the utmost of our being - it is a year-long gasp factor. And I suppose that's why so many *britanniques* join in our luck. Why not join them? I'm going to finish with a poem written, strangely, enough by that pretentious brit who calls himself the ymmygrant. Personally I thought it rather good, but then I would wouldn't I?. Village of dreams. Nice one ymmygrant. Even stranger he wrote it also in French. Bloody show-off.

Eus – Village of Dreams

If you travel to Prades on the main promenade
Just look from the road to the right
A vision appears your lethargy clears
That's Eus the village of light

The houses bestride the steep mountainside
A Canigou view is the jewel

They cascade from the sky and seem to defy
Gravity's unbreakable rule

The church at the peak displays the mystique
Of an angel adorning a tree
The whole gives the sight of eye-catching delight
And beckons you there urgently

So you free mental chains along country lanes
Taking a moment to glance
At an impressive sign as you reach the incline
'A beautiful village of France'

You climb to road's end through tight hairpin bends
To park where you can go no more
You're now near the top, where you must stop
From now you will need to explore

You look at the view of the bold canigou
Still wearing his top-hat of snow
The sight is resplendent, almost transcendant
It sets all your senses aglow

So now start the search for the old baroque church
A journey that's well worth the climb
If you enter inside there may be a guide
The interior is truly sublime

Descend to the square there's good coffee there
A haven of peace and respite
Before you explore the village once more
In the sun's all-encompassing light

Descending some more through ruelles galore
Tunnels and bridges as well
Pale pink achillea and blue bougainvillea
Cast an agreeable spell

At the foot of the hill so tranquil and still
A church that's a thousand years old
Colourful blooms bedeck silent tombs
It's a peaceable sight to behold

Up to the hall the melodious call

Of Cant-Eus the village's choir
Groups from four nations sing with elation
Songs from their rich repertoire

Each Easter Monday is the choir fun day
They sing songs for eggs in the streets
Soon they will break them and then they'll make them
Into omelettes for people to eat

Here feasting is rife, a homage to life
In an epicurean meeting
Whatever the weather the people together
Will find any pretext for eating

The village hall shakes like a dozen earthquakes
When the weekly rave-up is there
But when summer's here the dance will appear
Out in the old village square

As May ends its race and June takes its place
It's the annual art celebration
They come from afar to this croisée d'art
Because of it's high reputation

A village of music a village of art
A village of leisure and peace
A village with beauty and love in its heart
Where the rays of the sun never cease.

Enjoy your sojourn you'll surely return
To live with a sense of romance
Known through the nation for its reputation
'The sunniest village in France'

The Conflent Tales

Chapter the Twelfth

The

Culture Presydent's Tale

Being the tale of how high culture insinuated its way into Conflent life

The Culture President's tale.

Hello – my name is Jeanne and I'm the President of the local cultural and heritage committee. Red-headed, shapely, fun-loving, likes good books, travel and other things in the comfort of one's own home - looking for male of similar..... oops – sorry that's a slip of the memory and definitely not why I was asked to write this chapter. Still, if you're reading this and..... Let's restart. Now I remember, the *Culture et Patrimoine* bit, that's what they asked me to do.

Well, even in this part of what those Brits seem to think is Paradise, as in the real world, traditions have tended to fall by the wayside, overwhelmed by modern manners and mores, and television soaps. Young people no longer learn to speak their native language of Catalan, they use the glottlestops of modern French. Farmers don't use horses, they drive tractors, usually at a horse's pace, along mediaeval sized country lanes where overtaking is a pastime indulged in only by those with a suicidal tendency (of whom there are more than a few in this region). They install *helices*, large, noisy whirling blades that disturb the air to preserve the budding fruit during late frosts. At least it's better than the old tradition of lighting up iron polluting pots filled with used engine oil that left a massive pall of black, acrid odoriferous cloud above the whole valley, and propelled a few more respiratory patients into the local hospital, and sometimes the morgue. They then use their *atomiseurs* to pollute the same fruit trees liberally with powerful toxic materials and *desherbants* several times a month. If you people only knew what you are really buying for your kilo of peaches!

But that's by the by. The power of ancient custom is making a strong comeback, and that's mainly because of my intellectual talents. I have even formed a new committee and called it *'Eus Culture et Patrimoine'* to show off the heritage and re-animate the culture of the region. It is very popular with those who consider themselves to be a cut above the rest and that covers some of the Brits and most of the French, but don't tell them I said so. I, together with two other Brits, one Dutchwoman and several grave and committed fellow-French villagers are part of it, largely by dint of the fact that they happened to be around when the association was formed. In this respect, the French do not differ much from the English way of doing things - if you're present at the first meeting you're on the committee.

We have even given the Brits positions of responsibility. For example, Jim, a former bank manager, a sad and deluded man who says he supports Chelsea at Soccer, Kent at Cricket and England at Rugby Union - whatever that means - in la France profonde, sport is another world - is making his bean-counting skills available to it. He is its *tresorier* and his friend Eddie, for his sins is the *secretaire adjoint*, which means that he does the writing when the real secretary isn't there. Luckily for him, the committee and the French language, this has not yet happened and we have so far been spared the written version of pigeon-speak that passes for French among the British Community.

Every month, the committee attacks with gusto the twin businesses of providing intellectual stimulation against all odds in our little corner of the Conflent and force-feeding the villagers with their history. *Par exemple*, we hold a poetry competition, in which today's budding Baudelaires, Racines and La Fontaines cut their metrical teeth in both French and Catalan. Then the local lyrical wordsmiths deliver earnest lectures on the delights of iambic pentameter and avant garde verse to a surprisingly large audience, many of whom don't know an iamb from a dactyl, or even from a mountain goat. There I go again, dissing my flock of cultural wannabes. I can't help it sometimes. It must be because of my intellectual superiority. I'll try not to do it again.

Despite that, as a result of our activities, Eus has become the liveliest, and most cultured village in the whole of the Conflent, a very haven for sculptors, scribblers and artists, especially those who paint incomprehensible squiggles on the canvas and call it contemporary art. Oops again! Perhaps I wasn't supposed to say that, but then I personally am not a painter, except for the household doors and walls. Anyway, as I was saying, to proclaim our superiority to the world, we organise - I use the verb loosely, organisation is not a word in the lexicon of most catalans - a *'Croisée d'Arts'*. Sounds important? It surely is for those of us devoted to educating the masses in matters of culture! What it means is *portes ouvertes* throughout the village for anyone who sculpts, paints, finger draws, throws pots, makes jewellery or farts in colour. This is when we discover what a hothouse of artistic endeavour lies within the village boundaries - an indicator of its true soul. Every inhabitant who has ever contemplated painting, even if only the kitchen door, seems to find something to exhibit (sometimes it *is* the kitchen door), and those who, like me, are spatially and aesthetically challenged in the visual arts, allow others to use their houses to hang paintings, display newly thrown crockery, demonstrate arcane arc-welding techniques, show bright and shining new artefacts and decorate windows with prettily coloured glass objects.

First stop for the croisée d'arts

People flock from miles around to view, gaup, wonder, admire, marvel, stupefact and sometimes, rarely, even to put their hands in their pockets and buy. The wife of Eus is one of the many who display their paintings at the *Croisée d'arts* and this year, I think I heard her mumbling under her breath about the stinginess of the visitors. Nevertheles, stingy or not, it's certainly popular. Last year the narrow road up to the top of the village was 2 deep in cars and the cavalcade of visiting vehicles extended for miles beyond. It took 3 days to get the people trapped at the top out. That's what we intellectuals call a truth lapse of course, but it serves to make a point.

The *Croisee d'Arts* is the time too when we realise what a dangerous place the village can be. Take Albert for example. He lives in its very epicentre, and specialises in welding large pieces of metal into weird and mysterious shapes according to his whim of the moment. His atelier resembles something like a cross between a scrap metal yard and a mini iron and steel factory. When he is at work, blue, red and green sparks fly psychedelically and randomly in all directions, while in his yard outside lies enough oxy-acetylene raw material to blow the village into the stratosphere. It is fortunate that sangfroid is a french word since his neighbours seem to have a superabundance of the stuff. Or perhaps that's why they go to pray in the church twice as often as the others. Arc-welding is after all his *métier* and that is what counts.

There are other worthy activities. One of them takes the eccentric view that real history is in the hearts and minds of the older people, who are represented in the village in copious numbers. And so we have a drive to transfer their memories and experiences onto audio-tape with an intention to compile an epic of Eus's living history. We actually thought that this could be a great learning experience for the kids, and manufactured a plan to have hordes of school-children knocking on ancient doors, enthusiastically waving their tape-recorders at bemused third, fourth and fifth-agers. Alas it was not to be. The French school system and, more appositely, the fact that there are only 3 children in the village of an age to interview - and one of *them* is only 3 years old - defeated that *grande idée.* However, each Tuesday afternoon in the *Maison du Temps Libre*, the village wrinklies are to be seen eyeing the high tech of a tape recorder with undisguised suspicion, as if it were one of Satan's anvils, and speaking hesitantly to *Madame la Présidente* (that's me) herself. After a few minutes to come to terms with the idea that I am not from the tax office or the social security, and nor am I the guardian of the Styx come to take them across, they break into an unstoppable diarrhoea of voluble reminiscing, providing the raw data for 20 volumes of fascinating village history, and perhaps the TV rights to a 30 episode mini-series. That has the potential to be as gripping (or boring depending on your point of view) as Eastenders. I saw that programme once when I was England and not even the Eus villagers could be as sad or dysfunctional as that bunch of squabbling losers. Sorry, I just couldn't help showing how I am so much more knowledgeable of high culture than you clueless peasants who live in the real world. I'll try to curb it in future. But it's difficult!

One of my many personae in the activities of *culture et patrimoine* is to act as its musical soul. Every year I organise a visiting ensemble, - a choir, a band, a gaggle of singers - to perform in the church or the village hall, feeding from the international festival at Latour de France whose director I know. I enlist the other *Britanniques* in the process. It is a labour of considerable love, not least in the generation and distribution of publicity materials to make sure that people turn up. We have had some marvellously magical musical evenings. Last year saw the visit of a young brass band from a village called Astley, not 7 miles from the town where Eddie, the immigrant, was born in Lancashire. Now I know that the wife of Eus has mentioned this band but I can't help telling it like it was, because I'm the intellectual and she's only, well, the wife of Eus, and Eddie as it happens. The kids were anything from 6 to 16 and led by an ebullient and highly gifted young bandleader called Helen Minshall. At this point I should mention that the Eus village hall is not exactly a shed in an adjoining muddy field as tends to be the case in many British villages. It is in fact a superbly designed Pyrennean-Scandinavian structure situated at the summit of the village overlooking the whole of the Conflent valley. It confronts the Canigou with some defiance, confidently matching nature's beauty against human inventiveness. Its terrace affords one of the most stunning views in Europe.

It was on this very terrace that I and my co-cultural conspirators placed the 50 or so members of the band, while inside sat the 200 plus punters in the audience who had paid the entrance fee of zilch to get in. (Our marketing strategy leaves nothing to chance. But *'entrée gratuite'* doesn't say how much it costs to leave!). So against the backdrop of the twinkling lights of Prades in the middle distance and the imposing outline of the mountain opposite, these youngsters proceeded to give us the most exquisite demonstration of brass band music ever heard in the Conflent. 6 year old Jack Brymers, 8 year old Benny Goodmans and 10 year old Gerard Hoffnungs (that dates me!) played their hearts out, inspired by the idyllic setting, the enthusiasm of the audience and the balminess of the evening. The whole concert was an entrancing, entertaining, engaging, magical, marvellous, mystical experience, reserved only for those who had the great good fortune to be there. They played Gershwin and Goldoni, Bart and Bach, Crosby and Corelli. Their last rendition of New York, New York had half the audience dancing at the back of the hall and the other half in full Sinatran voice. Before leaving, the audience contributed almost £300 to the cause of new instruments for the band. Now, *that's* what *'entrée gratuite'* means in this part of the world.

More prosaically, after the show the famous *britannique* ladies cooked a mountain of beefburgers on an open fire, ladled tons of onions, heaved gallons of tomato ketchup onto them and handed them out to the performers. These were washed down with copious quantities of dioxin-free Coke and followed by some of the most luscious peaches these children had ever seen. The French helpers amongst us looked on in perplexed amazement - that children who could produce such divine music could also consume such disgusting food will always remain one of the many anglo-saxon mysteries for them. As a result of this magical evening, the Wigan Town pennant still hangs proudly in the Eus village hall. I doubt that any of our villagers will ever get to that paradise of South East Lancashire to reciprocate the visit, but we luxuriate in the knowledge that, somewhere in Wigan, probably in a recess of the grandly named Astley Miners Welfare hut, there lurks a poster of the *village perché* of Eus, and fifty memories of an evening that will linger long in the mind.

Loussier set loose

I have one other claim to musical fame and that is that I have actually shaken the hand of the great Jacques Loussier, whose trio became, in the late 1960s, synonymous, along with the Modern Jazz Quartet, with the best there is in this genre We mourned with the rest of his admirers when he escaped this world into a Tibetan monastery in the late 1970s, and rejoiced when he emerged at the end of 1980s apparently none the worse for the experience.

I could have, if I had wished and been able to, paid 100 euros and more to hear the trio play in Paris, New York or London. Imagine therefore my surprise and delight when they consented to play Bach at a Boris Vian Foundation concert in our village hall - for 5 euros. This was a cultural occasion not to be missed, a feast of self-indulgence.

And so it turned out. Loussier, hands now caressing, now dancing mercurially over, the ivory keyboard, teased delicate inspiration from the empty air, Charbonnier on the double bass plucked melodies and rhythms that Bach had never thought of and Arpino brought forth a stupendous variety of sounds from anything which had the temerity to stand in the way of his whirling drumsticks. Now that's what I call intellectual-speak! Creative isn't it?

My cousin, a musical philistine of the first order, joined me at the concert. He went on sufferance and because his wife nagged him to go, and had to take their 11 year youngster rather than leave him alone in a strange home. They both expected to be bored silly, but their expectations were not to be realised. Instead my cousin ended up standing on his seat after each number, shouting and cheering louder than the rest of audience put together - and they were by no means silent. The life ambition of the 11 year old is now to be the next Jacques Loussier. And long may he prosper. The night was genial, the stars were in their heaven, the music was celestial and, as William Wordsworth might have said, bliss was it in that moment to be alive. You can see that, as a superior intellectual, I read British poetry as well.

Tradition, Tradition!

Enough of culture of the musical kind. Let my intellectual genius tell you about the APLEC, a *fratalan* word, meaning a sort of giant open-air encounter group in which villagers from four Communes take to the hills to fraternise and pray together in a romantic spot. Organising this is another of my humble responsibilities.

Each Monday of Pentecost (that's Whit Monday to you northern cannibals), the Eus villagers make a pilgrimage to the other half of the commune. If this sounds bizarre, there is a perfectly rational explanation. The full name of the commune over which I preside is *Eus et Comes*, although in terms of population the latter tends to have fallen behind - it boasts a population of precisely 2 sheep farmers. This is partly because most of the buildings in Comes have neither complete walls nor any roofs. It is in other words in a state of some dilapidation and fully justifies its Catalan name of Coma, since it spends most of the year sleeping. It is also several kilometres up the mountain from Eus and hence the pilgrimage.

At about 9 am the hardy souls of our village congregate in the Car Park near the Mairie at the top of the village. This being France, with the obligations of individual welcomes to perform, my brave band of brothers and sisters, commences the tortuous climb up the winding gravel road at about 9.45. At 10 it stops, already breathless, the average age of the village being well over 60, to admire the view over Prades from the bench 300 yards into the walk and to *bavard* a little more. Ten minutes later, audaciously pursuing their next objective, they arrive at the entrance to a dilapidated vignoble, the owner having thrown off this mortal coil some 10 years ago and his abundant heirs not having a clue what they should do with it. Here they rest again. This stop-go cycle, which mirrors the economic fortunes of the region and also their interest in things cultural, continues for the next 2 hours, until the mission is accomplished and the pilgrims, now members of a crocodile extending some 800 metres along the track, each make their own triumphant entry into the stony wreckage of Comes.

Meanwhile, the fainter hearts, pleading the necessity to act as pack mules, have left the same starting point by car and arrived at the same place by a circuitous route with everyone's special bag and the necessary accoutrements and ammunition for a barbecue and grill, including of course tables, chairs, cushions and games. With the arrival of everyone except the very slowest there is a collective sigh of triumphant satisfaction and a long lingering look out over the stupendous view across the crystal clear valley to a still white-topped Canigou framed majestically against an azure cloudless sky.

But first, since this is a cultural occasion, I arrange for the hordes to explore the ruined village of Comes and to reflect, as amateur Gibbons (the man, not the monkeys, though the level of knowledge is closer to the latter), on its decline and fall. As long ago as the 18th century it was a thriving community, if by thriving we mean the ability to remain barely alive despite the deprivations of such an exposed environment. Some 300 resolute individuals inhabited the now lifeless cottage shells and eked out a poverty-stricken living tending vines, herding cows and sheep and growing the sort of crops which could a) resist the extremes of a climate at 4000 feet b) grow roots in 2 inches of soil and c) provide a minimum of 800 calories a day. In my mind, not a vast dietary input but the wine helped to alleviate the hunger. There was never a huge number of dimensionally challenged people in Comes.

Some of the graffiti on the ancient church tell us who some of these people and their ancestors were and the rest are chronicled meticulously in the parish records of Eus. It's clear to me, as one of the more intelligent types, that they seem to have been extremely hopeful people. Wonderful christian names abound in the records. Bonaventure for example. I can imagine that someone born with such an eponymous title could be nothing other than a swashbuckling peasant-soldier of fortune, slashing the vines and slapping the cows in gay hedonistic abandon. The reality of course Is that the number of buckles to be swashed in a place like Comes was strictly limited. But perhaps he was able to share his devil-may-care philosophy with another of the villagers, Elysee. A name like that, reminiscent of the sybarytic self-indulgence of those fields which gave their name to a boulevard far away in my nation's capital, should signify perpetual pleasure and sensual delight. The prosaic truth is that there was precious little to smile about in olden-times Comes. Children, some of them contemporaries of my father, walked four kilometres down the mountain to go to school come rain, hail or shine, and wended their weary way elegaically homewards (note the subtle intellectual reference to another British poet – Thomas Gray) every evening. Life was tough, a constant battle against summer wind and winter cold and perpetual drought.
It was the last of these three which finally saw the end of the village. Seven successive years of rainless *sècheresse* in the 1920's finally saw the last of these hardy people retreat down the mountain to the fleshpots of Eus and Prades, and their families are now dotted around the lower valley. In past centuries even this would not have been an option open to them, and the lonely cemetery bears silent witness to hundreds of souls taken unwillingly before their time.

But at least they had their religion and this was a great part of their culture. The Church is the only building now still standing with a roof. Its romanesque shape and its dry-stone walls betray its date of construction around the 10th century and, for me, there is a sad beauty in the simplicity of its lines. Inside, it is equally sparse and bare, though not severe, since traces of deep blues and rich reds dating back many hundreds of years can be seen on its crumbling plaster walls. Some of this sparseness is due to the devastation caused by passing bounty-hunters, who have stolen just about everything that could be moved, including the altar and some of the ornate grave stones in the cemetery. The altar rail though is still in place, standing guard over the raised stone platform of the chancel where once stood a succession of country priests preparing communion at the altar table. It must have been a place of great faith and great solace in times past. In the present I can only say that its appearance displays not just the sad remembrance of times past and people forgotten, but also the sickness and decadence of our age. Now that's an intellectual comment if you like!

The Romanesque church of Comes stands above the ruined village

Like many local customs, the APLEC has its roots in religion. The people of the four communes like nothing better than an open air mass to celebrate the confirmation of the rising of their saviour into heaven. Up above the valley so high, one can almost believe that many of them are half-way there already. Mass is scheduled for around 11 am catalan time, and so at 11.30 a large group of people gather round a make-shift altar table, a statue of the Virgin Mary is hoisted aloft and the two duty priests start the catechism. The air seems to become still; the bees seem to stop buzzing, the birds apparently stop singing, the crickets stop playing cricket while the sounds of worship fill the countryside. The best singers from the villages sing, the priests chant, the congregation responds, and the Brits look on in wonder. The view across the valley is stupendous. God is in his perfect heaven and nothing can possibly go wrong with the world in this perfect place. That is until the next item on the APLEC calendar takes place, for which I claim no responsibility, since my part as cultural czarina in the proceedings, is now complete. But I'll describe them anyway in my own intellectual, and therefore unreadable, style. But persevere, you peasants!

A snow-topped Canigou surveys the scene across the valley

Back on the field below the village the festivities, and the pork chops and sausages, are in full flame. Small islands of people sit around the tables they have commandeered, surrounded by refrigerated boxes and crates of wine, eagerly tucking into the hors d'oeuvres they have plundered from a central table. It comprises a potato salad, laced with beans, mushrooms, peppers and olives with what seems like a green mountain of lettuce leaves. As I might have foreseen, only one group is table-less, preferring to slum it with the ants, beetles and other creatures of the field. This of course is the British contingent, courageous to the end, chins thrust forward defiantly and upper lips starch-rigid. They have eschewed the little niceties and comforts of our French barbecue life such as tables and chairs in favour of the obligatory British-blanket-on-the-ground and bums in God-knows-what on the grass. At least they have the ironmongery and crockery even if it takes a superhuman effort to twist the body into shapes it was never designed to adopt in order to access the nourishment. But *tant pis* for them, the *merguez* are now nicely black, the pork chops are similarly coloured, and both are available at the big central table, together with a catholic selection of appetising sauces.

What is more important, so are the crates of red and rose wine, which are the only civilised accompaniment to any meal in France, and an appropriate way to convert chronic discomfort into acceptable ease. Thus fortified, everyone says no to the fifth chop and the tenth sausage and swiftly consigns the cheese course and dessert - the first peaches and cherries of the season - to oblivion. Normally, such consummate gastronomy is succeeded by the luxury of a siesta in the reclining chair, and indeed there is a marked diminution of conversational chatter as replete bodies wriggle and writhe in quest of a comfortable position. The first incipient snores of forgetfulness might even be discerned by the indiscreet listener.

But such idyllic dreams do not last. As everyone of us has experienced, there are always those, especially from among the barbarians of more northerly climes, who simply cannot relax even for ten minutes, and who just happen to have found a frisbee in the bottom of their picnic hamper. That a plastic saucer-shaped object should provide the focus for so much fevered activity and hysterical laughter in the lower field might seem to be unbelievable, but the wine has done its work well and spirits are high. In addition they no longer need to endure their *tête à tëte* with the local bugs. As the sleepers awake, they too join in, until the Spirit of the Canigou, looking timelessly across the valley for signs of intelligent life, would survey an assemblage of the world's greatest and most cerebral of species cavorting noisily in happy circles under the windworn walls of the ruined village. And it would, from that moment, know that flying saucers are, together with the origin of species, writ large into the ancestral spirit of mankind.

Later, he (for Canigou is assuredly male, and macho with it) would see, and ponder in wondering incredulity, the spectacle of these same resourceful and logical beings producing spherical iron projectiles to organise – again one uses the word loosely - that most French of pastimes, a *concours* of *boules*. The process of assigning the planet's most rational brains into two equally competent teams is a simple one. Each participant throws one boule towards a small bright object in the middle distance and, this task having been accomplished, those furthest away from it play against those nearest to it. If the Canigou were aware of a more equitable way of doing this, he wasn't saying. Then would follow the familiar *petanqual* cries of '*tirez*' and '*pointez*' and '*C'est pas vrai* and *Catastrophe*!' Anglo-gallic hands would be anglo-gallically wrung and exasperated glances cast to the unsympathetic skies, expletives of triumph and expletives better deleted would be directed across the valley to the imaginary thousands in the stands fashioned from the vast bowl of the mountains. The standard-bearers of two of humankind's greatest cultures pass resolutely and anxiously from one end to other and back again until the game is ended and the winners acclaimed.

Thus fulfilled, and having victoriously filled the empty chasm of the day, at 5 pm the blissful and exhausted throng homeward wends its weary way down the mountain-side, and relates heroic tales of a supremely successful event to those they left behind. I of course, as always, modestly refrain from accepting the praise for yet another cultural triumph. There is always another one for intellectual types like me to organise next week, next month, next year. Meanwhile if you're looking for a good time with special equipment, black leather and „„ oops there I go again! Sorry.

The Conflent Tales

Chapter the Thyrteenth

Mort D'Artur.

Mort d'Artur

Artur is gone. No words can describe the desolation we feel at the suddenness of his passing. Nothing can ever refill the now empty hole in our hearts in which he had spent eleven years etching his own special brand of humour and his unconditional love. We look for him in the mornings in his usual place on the patio and the space he occupied is empty. We listen for his welcome bark as we return to the house and the air is silent. Our fingers ache to bury themselves in his magnificent coat and they touch an unfilled void. Only time can heal the grief and the loneliness we feel at this time.

Artur had a way of forcing entry to the hearts of others too. Heads turned wherever he went. Appreciative gasps of 'Quel beau chien' or 'magnifique' from a succession of admirers as he walked proudly along the street, or cavorted happily in the fields, bought for him short-term honour. And he knew it - oh how he knew it! He pretended indifference while silently preening his own beauty. But for those who had the pleasure of meeting him more frequently and knowing him more intimately, the process was much more subtle and insidious. While my wife was clearly number one in his affections, he admitted others into his heart and played the 'love me' card for all it was worth. Our friends became victims of his beguiling personality. Even those who affected to dislike dogs could see that this one was different. The mocking sense of humour, the meaningful look, the secret nuzzle, the knowing tongue-wagging laughter, all part of a carefully planned design to transform unwary humans into Arturian swains .

One could look into his deep red eyes behind the acres of wool and see not the vacant stare of a dog but the deep-seated, uncommunicable wisdom of generations of Briards. He seemed to know what we were thinking before we thought it ourselves. He mourned with us in our times of sorrow, he remonstrated silently with us when we argued and he laughed with us when we were happy. I swear too that he manipulated our moods to his own advantage. When we were sitting down in the evening, he would trot self-consciously up to us and direct his gaze upon our faces as if looking for a clue to our mood of the moment. Disinterest, unhappiness, boredom, these were not allowed - only the spontaneous expression of pleasure and its shared gratification with him was permitted. He was an unreconstructed hedonist, making no apologies for forgetting the cares of this modern world or the pain of those more unfortunate than him.

And yet when pain came he was patience personified. The constant invasion of tics, grass seeds, broken glass, pebbles and twigs into his paws and his coat was a nuisance but one to be endured and remedied by his mistress. He would lie resignedly on his side while my wife, armed with a vast array of instruments of canine torture, cleaned his wounds and administered painful mercy. He did not bite her when hurt, nor would he ever. She was his nurse, his surgeon, his mother, his Goddess, and in all things she was completely infallible. His faith in her knew no limits.

For her his loss is huge. He was her constant companion during my frequent business absences, he was her 'beau bébé', the grand-child she craved for and did not have, he was the dog she had never owned in her childhood, he was the object of her devotion. In him she invested endless hours and endless care. As for Artur, his only objective in life was her security and her happiness. He lived to please her. They were almost inseparable - twin souls, animal and human, for eleven glorious years of the continuum that is eternity.

Artur did not spend all his life in one place as many Briards do. He was a traveller – a late 20th century European explorer. Born in Normandy with English owners, he lived in Paris, Brussels, Eus in the Conflent and even in England after a harrowing, and totally unnecessary, 6 months in quarantine. He happily occupied hotel rooms in Italy, Switzerland, Holland, Germany, Spain, Scotland, Wales and Austria.

Images of his happy and crowded life abound. Artur, at 4 months already a hefty 10 kilos, separating himself from his 2 brothers and choosing us, quite dispassionately, as his life partners. Artur in our Paris flat, ears glued back for ten months as his distinctive Briard appearance took shape. Artur, the king of his young playground realm, the Bois de Boulogne, playing regally with his subjects as they too emerged from the surrounding apartments. Artur, the emperor of the Foret de Soignes near Brussels, chasing the rabbits and the chipmunks, and though he never caught up with one, returning happy from the morning's hunt - once finding himself confronted unexpectedly by a 3 metre ditch and clearing it with a prodigious leap which drew applause from everyone who saw it.

Artur, locked in the prison of the english quarantine kennel, subtly interposing himself between us and the door to make sure that we did not leave without him - and the look of betrayal on his face as we did. Artur in his prime, Lord of the New Forest, strutting majestically across heath and heather. Artur, bounding up the stairs of our 3 storey farmhouse in the Conflent and clattering down it at breakneck speed, hoping to do a spot of ethnic cleansing on the cat. Artur, now more mature, trotting sedately around the Vinca lake and around the lanes of Las Pharaderes, surrounded by the organ-destroying, fruit-farming pollution which would eventually contribute to his death.

He had a fetish for socks, the sweatier the better. No visitor ever escaped without at least one sock having had the Artur treatment, and my wardrobe is still full of single items because the other has an Arturian hole at its toe or its heel. After socks in his popularity poll came knickers, and then handkerchiefs which he would tear to myriad pieces with great and exaggerated gusto. Prades market benefited hugely from these delightful habits.

Recurring images of Artur's magnificent physique. Permanently enveloped in a long beige woolly overcoat with touches of black, a mane which would have graced the proudest lion, one of the finest tails in the history of the Briard, an enormous imposing head emphasising the impression of great strength of character, eyes of the deepest red and a coat which presented an insurmountable challenge to the best of canine coiffeuses.

But most of all the images are of his personality. Proud, indefatigable, loving, wise, lovable, faithful, humorous, determined, patient, sometimes sulky, boisterous, enthusiastic, fun-loving, intelligent, imposing, noble, majestic. Add the superlatives as you will - they will not convey the half of what Artur really meant to us. He was 'le roi Artur' - the hero who lives on in legend in both France and England and who will never die from our memory.

He lies at rest down by the stream among the trees and the plants of the glade. It is a fitting place. He will forever dream his dreams - of steaming socks and catchable cats, and forests as far as the Briard eye can see - near to the place where he spent the last happy days of his happy life.

One last image remains, forever burnt into my psyche. While lying unmoving in his last, laboriously hewn, resting place by the stream, Artur's back legs protruded slightly from the grave. Maggie, despite her overwhelming grief, gently took them into her hands and placed them comfortably under his body. She then stroked him for the last time and said ' There now, old fellow, you enjoyed lying like that didn't you' - We could almost feel his last reply as we covered his lifeless body with the rich Roussillon earth, 'Thank-you mistress - thank-you for a wonderful, wonderful life.'

Artur du Clos de L'Ante, Briard, born Falaise, Normandie 18 May 1985, died peacefully Eus, Pyrenées-Orientales 24 July 1996.

Rest in Peace, old lad, and thank you for the bountiful pleasure you gave to all you came into contact with, and especially for your unselfish enrichment of our lives. We are proud to have known you.

The Conflent Tales

Chapter the Fourteenth

The Hunter's Tale

A Tale of Bravery, Valour, Daring, Heroism and Courage in the Face of Great Peril

The Hunter's Tale

Hi, my name is Jean and I am a bold, brave hunter. Killing wild animals is the raison d'être of my existence. I risk life and limb every weekend and Wednesday between August and February when the hunting season is in full flow. Me and my mates are a happy band of brothers. Shooting bullets at helpless wildlife helps to keep us cheerful in the dark winter days when there isn't much else to do. That and annoying our non-hunting brethren when we're in hot pursuit of our quarry. We have rights, you see. We can follow them onto other people's gardens and even into their houses if that's where the stupid animal decides to go. That's what comes from having a *'chasse et pêche'* representative in the French Parliament to look after our interests. And to help us implement our ruthless task, we have artillery and the right to bear arms. Not quite like the USA where, under the constitution, they can have tactical nuclear warheads if they so wish. That's what I, and my mates, call real firepower. If only I could get my hands on an AK assault rifle –that would be enough for me. But successive spineless French Governments have whittled away our French right to terrorise our neighbours and enemies. Whatever, why dream? The weaponry at our disposal is still considerable. Knives that a London Street Gang would give up an eye for. Guns that would make a Taliban tribesman salivate. Well, we need all the help we can get in our mission to rid the country of every living wild animal.

Oops, did I just write something I shouldn't have? We actually tell the Government that our purpose in life is to keep the environment pure and free of surplus animals and birds like pigeons, ducks, rabbits, wild boar and deer. In fact we are doing the state a big favour and totally for free. Well, that's what we tell the Government and the gullible folk who live in the villages and towns. But we know that there's nothing like the excitement of pulling the trigger on a *sanglier* and the blood-lust after a kill. Brings a real adrenalin rush to the heart and a sense of peace to the soul, not to mention an increase in the saliva glands in the anticipation of a good square meal. We go to Church afterwards of course to confess that we're sorry, but the priest seems to think that it's all part of God 's great purpose, and who are we to argue with that?

Pathetic Brits

You wouldn't find us dressing up like raspberry tarts as they do in England. Forelock touching went out with the revolution. And anyway that's not real hunting. Poncing about on horseback, blowing horns and looking for foxes for the dogs to tear apart, isn't really our style. Barbarian if you ask me, primitive, archaic, antediluvian. But what can you expect from a race that burned an innocent young girl like our beloved *Jeanne d'Arc* at the stake? We fearless French hunters will have none of it. And nor will we have any of that anti-hunt nonsense they have to suffer up there. Any liberal-minded townie prat who starts to spray pepper near me gets the first barrel up his jaxi. Justified retaliation. And we hear they're not even allowed to perform that disgusting fox ritual now (though we also hear that a blind eye is turned). What the hell are the brits coming to? Dragging a fox-scented piece of cloth around the countryside just to give the hounds some exercise doesn't exactly have the same redolence if you see what I mean. They'll be looking for gun control next. Come to think of it they already have. Knives too. Lily-livered wets. Hope it isn't catching.

Now we brave and manly French hunters prefer to create our carnage silently and with precision. We leave rabbits and the small fry to the amateurs who don't know any better. We macho men will only make war on the big stuff, and in particular, in the absence of grizzlies in these parts, the boar. You wouldn't want an enraged 200 kilogram male monster pig charging at you at 80 kilometres an hour, I can tell you. Happened to me only once when I went up the track to relieve myself of the beer sloshing around inside. Naturally I didn't have my gun in hand – one doesn't in these circumstances. Anyway I was in mid-stream, so to speak, when I looked up and saw this leviathan bearing down on me at a high rate of knots. This is not the time to take a careful analysis of the situation, nor even to zip up. So there I was, bits flapping about, making a beeline to the nearest tree. It was only by shinning up it that I escaped certain death. I completed my ablutions on the pig below which didn't put him in any better mood. That'll teach him not to mess with brave Catalan hunters. Bloody embarrassing it was! I could hear my mates sniggering away in the bushes, until the brute turned its attention to them. If I'd had my trusty rifle a .23 bullet up its snout would give it enough of a headache to make it think twice. But my mates had the situation in hand. Fifty bullets later, there it was dead, a silent testimony to the folly of attacking brave and heroic hunters when they do have access to their weapons. When I came down from my tree, I got a real ribbing, but I smiled it off by pretending that it was a deliberate ploy to lure the pig to their guns.

Catalan hunters have a certain reputation for shooting the hunter rather than the hunted. It's all of course a lie made up by the pusillanimous sob-sticks who are trying to hinder those of who us enjoy using our weapons of destruction as a recreation. Though it's strange to me how our numbers keep dwindling from August to February, when we're allowed to make a complete take-over of the countryside. I put it down to gun fatigue. It can catch a fellow when he's not prepared. That and bossy wives who don't know their place. Mind you, several of my mates are often walking a bit stiff-legged by November. Don't like to ask why. Could be just a bit of stiffness, though that doesn't explain the wounds.

Many of the pathetic protesters I was mentioning are those perfidious Brits who complain about not being able walk their dogs without being potted at by a hidden hunter. It isn't our fault that they have dogs – we've got a few of our own with bells round their necks to root out the *sangliers*, and *they* don't get shot at. Well not much – we only lost about 30 of them last season, and some of those had psychiatric problems with the sound of the bells every time they moved their heads. Hunting dogs aren't what they used to be. And as for not being able to walk their dogs, what do they think Monday Tuesday, Thursday and Friday are for? Even on hunt days we put out warning boards that tell them not to advance a step further. When we remember of course. Otherwise they're fair game.

Dispersing the product

Which brings me to my next beef. When we do manage to get a lucky shot into the right place, we aren't allowed to sell the meat - Government regulation number whatever to make sure that it doesn't become a commercial activity, so they say. But *ve haf vays* as they say in our neighbouring country, and while you won't see our products on the butcher's shelf, a discreet whispered request might produce the required goods from the back room. Don't wear an inspector's uniform when you do. And a goodly number of polticians locally have been sweetened up with the brown paper packet they find on their back porch from time to time. But our major marketing event is when, once a year, we have a party for the villagers. This is where the wild boar meat is cooked into a delicious stew and served with potatoes. They love it – the best way to make French people say *Oui* is to satisfy their stomachs. After that we can continue to slaughter everything in sight at will. By the way, the other part of the strategy, in case there are any waverers, includes the mention of knives and guns.

More gutless Brits

The bane of my life is the gutless Brits who have started to infest the Conflent. Forever accusing us of invading their territory and spoiling their enjoyment of the countryside. Their territory indeed. This is France my friends and we are the only true Frenchmen. Take the boneless idiot who calls himself the Ymmygrant and that shrew, the Wyfe of Eus, as examples. They call us murderers, assassins, psychopaths, executioners, environmental primitives. They're right of course but I'm damned if I'll admit it to those saddoes. Not sure about the psychopath bit mind, I only want to kill animals and not humans – well not many of them – and they're mostly brits. But it makes my blood boil when I see them giving the pigs safe harbour near their houses, or shouting 'run, piggy, run' when I'm just lining up a shot between his ears. That should be a capital offence. It's taking the food from the mouths of their neighbours and the pleasure from us working class folk.

There was this time when I saw a young boar running like a demented dingo with diarrhoea in the direction of their house as if it was a pig refuge. Can't blame it for running really, since I had just shot and killed his mother. Anyway, as the whole world knows, young sanglier meat is far tenderer than that of the old sow I had just put to sleep permanently. It's a delicacy in these parts. So I was licking my lips in anticipation when the bugger disappeared. I know where it was. It was in their kitchen. I could hear it squealing away and the stupid wife trying to console it. But the door was locked. What to do? I thought of breaking the window and pointing my gun through it. Then I remembered that that same spiritless French Government had banned the shooting of guns within 50 metres of a dwelling place. What a weak, faint-hearted lot they are. If this was the USA I would have pointed my latest nuclear device straight at the house and annihilated the lot of them. But that would have defeated the purpose of providing the succulent meal I had in mind. So I adopted a subtle wait and see strategy. I stayed outside laying siege to the stinking house for 4 hours until it went dark. I could see them, peering through the shutters. I swear they were laughing at me, the pig honking away as well. Then in the twilight I had to give up. So I went to rescue the dead sow and, bugger me, if some thieving bastard hadn't picked it up and spirited it away. Ever since then I've hated the Brits for the weak-minded, cowardly, craven, double-dealing, duplicitous, treacherous boon-dockers they are.

A Hunter's Philosophy

If I had my way them bleedin' rosbifs wouldn't be here in my country. I'd have the machine gun nests at every port on *la Manche*. And the same goes for all them whackdottle foreigners - eyeties, dagoes, polskis, krauts, the lot of 'em. And as for the A-rabs. There aren't words for what I'd do to them. Le Pen's too much of a pussy-cat for me. If you ask me, and for some reason not many people do but I know they're thinking it, that Stalin had the right idea – those he didn't like he wasted. This country's going to the dogs. What we need is that little Corsican back. He sorted the buggers out, didn't he. Europe? No bloody way. Close the borders tight as a boar's bum. This is a dog eat dog world. You just have to look at them greedy bankers and company directors to understand that. They don't give a stuff about what anyone else thinks so long as they can line their pockets. And neither do I and a lot of my mates. That UKIP in rosbeefland's got the right idea. Turn the clock back to the time when Frenchmen were French and white-skinned, the empire gave up its loot to keep us comfortable and the foreigners only visited to tip shitloads of money into the national coffers and say how great your country is. And sod the future economy. Anyway that's what I think and if you disagree you shouldn't be reading this. I'll just keep on doing what I do best. Slaughtering animals.

Real French Hunting

Back to the story. Somehow I keep digressing, but that's what reasonable people like me do. A typical hunting day out will see me and my brethren decide where we want to hide ourselves. We are equipped with our armoury, and of course our lunch hampers to help sustain us during the hardships of the day. These will contain cold meats, perhaps including foie gras, chicken, salads, hams and of course copious quantities of wine and beer. At 12 precisely, after a hard morning peering through the foliage, the duty hunter will go back to the car and bring the tables and chairs without which we could not possibly consume this delicious feast. This would last perhaps 2-3 hours during which time 3 whole families of wild boar might have passed within a few metres. But this is France, my friends – everything in good place and good time.

The afternoon may start with a pleasant snooze among the trees and bushes before the serious business of animal slaying begins again. Most often there is no activity, but that does not worry us since there is always tomorrow, next week, next month. And we have dined well. But if that moment arrives when the dogs have disturbed a boar from his hiding place, we are ready for it. The guns point, the frisson of anticipation takes over, the triggers are pulled again and again in a fusillade of bullets aimed at bringing the fleeing boar down. Sounds like fireworks night on the 14th of July. At this point I have to say that we are not the greatest of marksmen. Most bullets miss their mark and are randomly scattered over the surrounding countryside. Woe betide any courting couple in the bushes or a passing runner out with his dog. They'll be visiting the hospital to have the pellets taken out of their bums – that is if they're still alive. We wouldn't object though if it was one those Brits. But, when all is said and done, it takes only one well-directed bullet to bring success to our endeavours. The enemy, usually, but not always, a wild boar. is dead. If the latter. we bring the van, load up our kill and return flushed with success to the village, where spaces have to be found in already stuffed freezers, or butchers unearthed to secrete the meat into their spacious back room. Thus ends a typical day, of which we see many.

Whatever happened to the Pig?

There seems to be one great drawback to my chosen sport. I regret to say that, strangely, the wild boar population in our area is falling fast, as is the occurrence of deer. I cannot think why this should be. Maybe pig fertility is not what it used to be. I wonder what happened to that *marcassin* that took refuge in the Brit's house. They've probably domesticated it like a dog and now it's barking. They're mad enough. Perhaps we now need him to re-populate the hills and bring back our opportunities to butcher his offspring. If you asked me why I became a hunter - was it a) an opportunity to make a contribution to the care of the natural environment in my region or b) an opportunity to feel good about killing wild animals, I would have to answer that it is certainly not the former. And the same would be true for most of my mates, but it's also the camaraderie that goes with our days in the hills, and a chance to spend a civilised day unencumbered by the wife.

So that's my tale. If it offends , I couldn't give a rabbit's rear end, especially if you are a Brit reading this. If you are, remember I've got a gun, a knife and a score to settle!

Post script

A Catalan Hunter rang the emergency line. 'Help, help' he said in panic, 'My buddy's just been shot. I think that he's dead.' The help line administrator said, 'Calm down, calm down sir. We can deal with this. But before I decide what should be done, please just make sure he's dead.' The hunter puts the phone down. She could hear his footsteps walking away. Then – a shot. Two seconds later, the hunter picks up the phone. He said 'OK. He's dead. What now?'

THE CONFLENT TALES

Chapter the Fyfteenth

The Wild Boar's Tale

Being the Confessions of a Wild Conflent Boar and his solution to the Problems of the Planet.

An Allegory for our Times

Hi. Greetings to you and your fellow humans from me, my female and all my little piggies – marcassins I think you call them in French. My name is Napoleon and I'm a sanglier – a wild boar to you barbarians from the North. I'm writing this on the hoof so to speak because there are a number of your species with psychopathic tendencies. They call themselves hunters – egos bigger than Africa and narcissistic and shameless to match. They seem to want to massacre me, my family and all my mates in the Conflent garrigue. I have not the faintest idea why, since we have done absolutely nothing to them that deserves such anti-social conduct. Seems strange to us. For 6 months of the year we are left in peace to do what us sangliers enjoy doing – eating the bounty of the earth, roaming from here to there in the hills, communing with nature in our own piggy way and debating the meaning of life on this planet.

Then, come August, boom. It's open season again for all the dimwits, peabrains, lunatics and sociopaths of the human race to gratify their tiny, belligerent minds by skulking in bushes so that they can shoot their ghastly guns at us. What on earth goes through their simple heads at this time? They have absolutely no respect for us sons of nature. And they call themselves the master race? There's more intelligence in my eldest son's bum than that lot put together. Take that witless neanderthal who calls himself the hunter. Brains of a dead newt, the morals of a serial abuser and the personal vision of a confused mole. Thinks he's France's answer to Vlad the Impaler with his fancy guns, his bigoted values and his bottles of booze. Half-drunk most of the time and couldn't hit an elephant from 12 inches. We have some fun with him I can tell you, senseless twit. We wait until he comes out of the undergrowth to relieve himself of all that liquid and leaves his artillery behind. Then while he's in mid-stream so to speak we make a guest appearance. Bit like shouting boo to an educationally sub-normal child. Scares him shitless. There is no finer sight in boar-lore than to see a human hunter-killer in full flight, pants round his ankles, shouting blue murder back to his mates. This one climbs up a tree for good measure. Gives us stitches laughing. Then we slip off quietly into the forest and let the stupid half-wits bang off their weaponry at nothing in particular. Must admit that all that noise isn't good for my delicate ears but it's worth it to see the buffoons waste all their bullets on fresh air.

Why do they do it? Do you ever see a sanglier, or any other animal, trying to commit mass murder on humans just for the fun of it? Do we even want to? True my brothers have been known to demonstrate irritation in rather strong terms from time to time. But that's only when the brainless buggers invade our territory and threaten our families. We've seen and heard what that lot can do to nature. Just because we live in back of beyond doesn't mean that we don't have a world-view and as a committee member of sangliers international I'm particularly involved. Digging up huge areas of our earth's surface and leaving it looking like the inside of a septic tank. Hacking down millions of acres of trees as if they were weeds in the garden. Polluting half the planet's surface with pesticides, herbicides, and every other kind of cide until it's killed every living thing in sight – including themselves in time. Turning the oceans into a thick fishless soup. Massacring millions of their own kind because they don't like their ideas, their religions, their faces or they just get in the way of their ambitions. And they call themselves intelligent! What a shower! Don't they know that the planet can't stand much more of this. Haven't they heard of ecology, sustainability, morality, ethics, decency, honour, virtue, integrity. Well, of course not, words like that don't seem to apply to that depraved bunch of egotistical planet wreckers.

They're not all like that. That would be being as simple-minded as they are. I know from my own experience that there are some of them with a slight hint of intelligence and who even fight for justice, right and honesty. Take those Brits down Eus way who saved my little son from a messy early death by harbouring him in their house. It's written in that half-wit, the hunter's tale. Shows real guts that. Despite that the canaryhead murdered one of my females. I owe him for that, and I will certainly have satisfaction. But it's all very well having a few humans with a moral conscience. Trouble is, the other thick-headed morons are taking us down with them. When the earth's ecology's descended into a barren wasteland, and it will if they don't mend their ways pronto, there'll be nothing left for us or our fellow animals to eat either. Inconsiderate clowns. They should be put into an asylum where they belong.

Now we sangliers have a code of conduct and a way of life that every one of us abides by. One that preserves rather than destroys. We build our own shelters from the bounty of the earth, fallen tree branches and dried grass, ravaging and exploiting nothing. We bring up our families to respect the land. OK, unwary ramblers might tread on our pooh but that's a minor irritation compared with the filthy garbage that those humans can leave everywhere they go. We drink the water from springs and streams in the garrigue, robbing no other creature of its right to drink from nature's plenty. We eat roots, tubers which we dig up ourselves and nuts, berries, leaves and seeds as well as maybe a few lizards, snakes and frogs that might be bothering us. We never, ever take more than we need for ourselves and don't try to make fast buck by emptying the earth of its natural resources like the humans do. Nor would we ever eat humans or our fellow animals – that's disgusting, revolting, beneath thinking about. So what's the game? How come these malicious criminals with rifles hate us so much? What is it in the human psyche that wants to slaughter, murder, butcher, execute innocent creatures? If their families were starving, I could perhaps understand, though murder is murder in anyone's book. But they do it for what they call sport. Sport my fanny! It's ritual slaughter by creatures with no moral compass. Personally I can only come to the conclusion that humans are an aberration in the earth's evolution.

I have heard tell that they believe that there are too many of us and so we have to be culled, whatever that means, so they think they are doing the environment a favour. Bully for them! What incredible bare-faced hypocritical cheek. What about humans, Seven billion and counting, pinching all the best parts of the planet's surface to grow their repulsive food, crowding out our animal friends from their ancestral hunting grounds, massacring elephants, lions and tigers by the thousands for some very dubious purposes. Which species is the deviant over-populated one, you tell me? No prizes for guessing right. The answer's obvious! Culling's too good for them, but luckily they're doing a pretty fine job in keeping their own numbers down by exterminating each other with their own weaponry.

Yes we dance a lot – we have a ball. Well we're a very happy breed. That's not just to celebrate our good fortune in being alive. It also disturbs the insects and uproots our food sources from under the ground. That's not anti-social behaviour, is it? We especially like to dance at night on flat green surfaces like gardens and what the humans call golf courses. My, how we really enjoy doing that. Then we hide in the woods and watch the groundsmen's faces when they inspect our work in the morning. That gives us a real thrill. What a colourful picture they are. There's a present up the jaxi to you from us!. I suppose it's one way of retaliating against the injustices we suffer. But it's nothing malicious you understand. Those are the sorts of terrain that have the best and most delicious food just underneath the soil – our gourmand delights you could say, a sanglier's epicurean experience. We also like to eat the grapes at the vendange time. That's led to more than a little ill-feeling I can tell you. But the stupid humans don't seem to have the brains to understand that other species have the right to eat, the freedom to roam, the liberty to bring up a family in peace. It's me, me, me all the time for them. That property's mine, those fields are mine, that forest is mine, that water is mine, that woman is mine. Like I said before, they're a malfunction in evolution. A danger to the future of the planet..

Now I'm not daft. I know that some animals like me also get into scraps for the territorial rights. But those repugnant bipeds take it to extremes. I've heard, I don't know how true it is because it's hardly believable, that they even slaughter thousands of their own kind at a time just to settle a quarrel. And it's not mano a mano. It's all done with technology – guns, drones, bombs and so on. How cowardly and spineless is that? When we sangliers want to settle a dispute we do it the noble way – male to male. Valour, courage and character are our watchwords, not this gutless, lily-livered combat from distance that humans practice. Indeed, it is written in the cultures of the Indo-European people, whoever they are – seems to me to cover a large slice of the earth's surface - that the sanglier is the embodiment of true warrior virtues. I saw that written down in a book (didn't you know we can read?) and it makes me very proud. It gets better. The same book said that, to the Celts, we were sacred. How about that – humans worshipping, instead of trying to exterminate, us. Now that's more what I had in mind. Apparently there was a Welsh hero called Culhwch who was reputed to be the son of a boar god. Boar (that's English for sanglier) GOD!. It's true that divinity fits very well into the sort of self-image I've had for some time. I might be pushing it a bit but I've always been subject to these mystical visions, especially after eating the local mushrooms. It must be a revelation of my innate spirituality. Not that those murdering bird-brains hiding in the bushes would ever notice. Seems to me that some of those old boys in history had more sense in their big toes than today's misguided delinquents with pop-guns.

Tell you what happened the other Wednesday – that's a licensed to kill day for the fearless hunters. We were wandering peacefully along a pathway known only to us in the garrigue – myself in the lead of course, my current favourite sow dutifully behind, followed by our 8 lovely striped marcassins.. I'm so proud of them. We were harming no-one in particular. Then we heard the sound of bells. Since it wasn't a Sunday we deduced (we're good at that Wild Boar Holmes stuff) that it was the dogs sent out by the hunters to flush us out so that, as usual, they could commence the slaughtering. We really feel sorry for those dogs – kept in small pens for most of their lives, half-starved to death and beaten if they so much as put a paw wrong. It's another sign of the primitive morals of the hunter race. Anyway I sent out the alarm and mum and the kids scattered into the sanglier hiding places, of which there are many in the garrigue, Now I have little arrangement with those doggies. We all have. When their owners are asleep in the dead of night we take them little titbits to eat. They're so grateful, the poor deprived famished creatures . The quid pro quo is that, whenever they find us, they lead the hunters in the opposite direction, preferably where the terrain is especially difficult and where there are precipices for their masters to fall over. We've chalked up a few successes on that score. So this they did, bells ringing merrily, while I went out in search of a hunter with his pants down so that I could give him a friendly poke up his nether regions. I didn't unfortunately find one this time out but the offer is always open. Later in the day we all met back at the sounder, where we celebrated our success with an extra ration of grubs and roots.

I have to admit though that we sangliers wouldn't win any prizes at an inter-animal beauty contest. Well, not under normal rules anyway. I have insight and I know that we're not the cutest of God's creatures. Even I can see that those nice-looking izards and even the mouflons with those monstrous curly ears would probably sweep the beauty board in this part of the world. But we sangliers do have family gatherings where the females express their admiration for the qualities that make us sangliers special. And that includes handsomeness as well as brute power. I myself have been voted the male most likely to for 3 consecutive years, and I have certainly fulfilled that expectation. I'm not sure about next year. There's a challenge from a strapping young hog in the offing for next rutting season and blow me if he isn't one my own offspring from 4 years ago. No point in appealing to his sense of filial duty. It just doesn't work like that, nor do I have any paternal obligations to him. I'll send the little sod packing if he isn't capable. Personally I think that his mother has put him up to it, ever since I gave her the old heave-ho for a younger model. That's how life is among us sangliers. The stronger gets his choice and the rest get the left-overs. A bit like human society nowadays, though it wasn't always like that with them. Maybe I'll pay his mum a visit after all. If I play it right she may just put in a good word for me.

But life isn't always about beauty and good looks. Put me in the forest glade with any one of those pretty boys up the hill and there's only one winner. And I include the humans in that, provided you take their weapons of mass destruction away. It's my dream to get any one of those sickos who call themselves hunters to a one-on-one duel among the trees – no armaments. I can see it all now – sangliers on one side of the ring and humans on the other, all cheering on their male favourite. The outcome of course is predetermined on weight alone (I weigh in at 250 kilos), though I would concede the option of allowing him to add lead to even things up. I wouldn't kill him of course – that would be bringing myself down to his level – but he wouldn't be sleeping with his wife for some time after, and any ideas about sitting down to a square meal would be wishful thinking.

I confess to having a bit of a temper when roused. All of us male sangliers have. When the red mist falls better look out. We're not responsible for our own actions. I suppose that we really ought to develop anger management courses, but they're not exactly our thing. But what would you do if a serial killer had just wasted your wife and a couple of kids? Understandable now, isn't it? So don't talk to me about curbing aggressive instincts. Anyway it only happens in the rutting season – the rest of the year we sangliers are just not in the mood. Not like those permanently randy sex-mad humanoids. Banging and bonking all the year through. Absolutely gross nauseating behaviour. No wonder the planet is over-crowded with the brain-dead stud-monkeys. I've said it before and I'll say it again. The planet can't support such obnoxious antics. It's only a relatively small rock in space. If we sangliers had the chance we would leave for another world in the universe where there is nothing but grass, grubs and tubers. No repulsive homicidal humans. Just sangliers. What a paradise that would be. I look up at the stars at night and let my mind wander. I know it isn't going to happen and those self-obsessed maniacs will eventually see us all extinct. But a boar can dream can't he?

One last word and it's in that book I was telling you about. The ancient Japanese admired sangliers so much that they named their sons after us. Blowed if I know how they knew what we were called but it shows that at least some of the humans had some intelligence in times past. We were even seen as symbols of fertility and prosperity. Makes me very proud that does. It also brings out the inborn creativity in me. I'm considering formulating a new economic theory that brings prosperity to every wild being, chickens, tigers, bees, elephants, aardvarks – all creation – except of course for the sponge-heads who would rather destroy the planet. Neo-sanglierism I think we'll call it and the universal unit of currency will be the boar. There will be none of this rich getting richer and poor getting poorer. Every wild beast will benefit from the natural bounty of the earth. Poverty will be eradicated. Education will be available to every creature – real creative education I mean, that opens up minds and widens horizons. Allows everyone to think and reason. Brainwashing by any source will be banned – it pervades every part of this world and it's distorted and twisted minds – filled them with hate. American TV, British tabloids, Madrassars, fundamentalist websites, nationalist movements and so on, So there will be no more of that!

What shall we do with the humans in my new world order? Well, they'll have to go I'm afraid. They've had their chance and they've botched it. They've simply got too greedy and lost the plot. Wrecked the climate, devastated the planet's surface, polluted the oceans, poisoned the soil, contaminated the atmosphere, destroyed the forests, annihilated the wild life, need I go on? Corporate profit came before common sense and the welfare of the planet. They and their kind will have to be eradicated or they will eventually eradicate us. So that's my recipe for the future to restore our beautiful planet to good health. In my world every creature will be equal – except for us sangliers. We will of course be more equal than the others. Thank you George for the idea.

Thank you for reading this. Might put it up on a petition site for wild animals – exterminate the humans, before they exterminate our planet and us with it.

Napoleon

The Conflent Tales

Chapter the Syxteenth

The Vicar's Tale

A cautionary tale of discovery, hope, progress, misunderstanding, betrayal and redemption.

Today's Sermon: It was lost and is found again

Hi, my name's Donald Blevins and Vicaring was my métier, as they say in France. Some (half)wit once called me Blev the Rev, and the name stuck, so, after throttling the fellow, I fell in and even put it onto my email address. (Yes, we spiritual types do indulge in modern-day technology, and No I am not going to give you the ultimate email address – that's private). The reason I'm writing this drivel is that a strange bearded guy approached me to write a piece for his book of Conflent Tales, and foolishly I agreed. Considering that I live a 5 hours drive from the Conflent it was a rum request, but it is true that I did spend some time visiting the region rather frequently of late, largely to bring the gospel to the district's assorted Anglicans. And, though they take some ministering to, and I can't now remember much about it, I have to say that I thoroughly enjoyed the blessed experience - I think.

So who am I? That's a question I sometimes have difficulty in answering myself. Thank the Lord for a clued-in wife. I retired some years ago from my Parish in Lesser Wittering by the Sea and came to France to recover and regain my sanity. In the last years it had suffered some buffeting from the winds of materialist change in the UK. The average age of my parishioners was something over 75. That was partly because the young people in the Parish had fled to more interesting places and, looking back on it now, the length of my sermons might have had some influence. Though Pride is one of the seven deadly sins, I did rather take great delight in ensuring that my flock was kept thoroughly informed about the totality of the scriptures and their significance for daily life. My record was 2 hours 7 minutes which I understand is also the record for running the marathon. One of the sheep, oops again, I must stop calling them that - one of my congregation, a particularly disagreeable and disagreeing type I seem to remember, told me that he would much have preferred to do the latter – he was one of the younger and friskier members of my flock at 78 years old and suffering from heart murmur. The others didn't comment, but I could tell that they were always concentrating very hard on the importance of what I was saying at the time because their eyes were tightly closed.

But now I'm reminiscing about times past. I must move forward into life as I live it in the present. Where am I? Oh yes, I remember, somewhere in France I believe, though I can never be certain nowadays. Aging vicar syndrome. So how did all this come about and why should a strange-looking person with a white beard ask me to write up my chronicle? Well, it's an interesting story, that's for sure.

In the year of our Lord 2005 I was holidaying with my wife in the area of Vernet les Bains, following in the footsteps of Kipling, so to speak. The day in question, one of the May days I recall, though I can't be sure, perhaps it was September, was fine and the air was crystal clear as mountain stream, to quote something whose provenance escapes me.

God was in his heaven and all was right with the world. I had just come from the town's Casino, where I was blessing the sinners within I hasten to add, on one of my daily perambulations, when I took an unaccustomed turning down a narrow lane and found myself confronted by a squarish stone building which looked uncommonly like a very English sort of church. On further examination, mostly achieved by peering through the keyhole of the door at its western end, I discovered that it was indeed a church. I could see the vague shape of an altar and a few pews. All was light inside since the gaps in the roof illuminated most of the building's interior. They reminded me of some of the houses that the estate agent showed us when we first came to France. Their own peculiar interpretation of open plan, lovely views of the sky, and so on. But I digress, as elderly vicars tend to do.

Where was I? Oh yes, the church. I was so excited, I can tell you, but I didn't rush into precipitate action. After all it could have been a false vision sent by Satan to test me. I am after all an aging vicar – or rather an aging ex-vicar – and a lifetime of describing miracles to worshippers for whom being alive was one of them, has left me wary of the consequences of inappropriate action.

So the following day I took the same walk, and this time brought my wife with me. She tends to be a little more of this earth than I. And, as we turned the corner, there it was again, unused, unloved and unendowed. The birds of the air and the fowl of the field (I may have that quotation wrong – sounds more like a football metaphor) could not have been happier than was I at that moment. It was as if I had discovered a new Jerusalem. Wiser counsel from my wife prevailed however. This is after all France, and this is a church in France. Not since before St Barthomelew's eve on the 24th August,1572, when Catherine de Medici massacred half the innocent protestants in France, have non-catholic churches been built in this benighted land. It is most likely to be a catholic look-alike built to entrap the unwary English who, according to local folklore, infested this place a hundred years previously.

So, wearing my best dog-collar, I went to the Mairie and enquired about its provenance. At first, they weren't very helpful. A trappist monk from the abbey of St Martin up the hill would have provided more information. They seemed to be, I have to say, extremely suspicious of my motives for asking, as if I were gathering intelligence to destroy the whole catholic faith in one fell swoop. Initially they denied its existence, saying that there was no such church in that place. But when I showed them a picture taken with my trusty mobile telephone and asked why it had an altar, the mayor's secretary reluctantly informed me that an Anglican church had indeed been built in the early 20th century, and that this was it. Imagine my joy on hearing this. A true revelation had been offered unto me. At the time, I now remember, it was Easter and I had a chance of a new resurrection – that of a truly Anglican congregation in a land of alien catholics. I must tell my friends, I must tell my colleagues, I must tell the world about this vision in ... where was I? Ah yes, in Vernet les Bains.

I'm not sure why, but my first thought was to inform the Headquarters of the Anglican church in the UK of my discovery. Surely they would be as thrilled as I was to know that the Anglican Faith had once been celebrated in a hill town in the Pyrennees. They would congratulate me for my powers of discovery and my prescience. I would present my plans for restoring the true faith in all its glory.

Alas, as it turned out, it was not to be a stimulating series of conversations, as you will see.

DB: Hello , is that the Anglican Headquarters
Anglican Headquarters : Well sir. it depends what you mean by Headquarters – we're not a military establishment or a corporate business.
DB: OK So what do you call yourselves?
AM: Well sir. We like to think of ourselves as God's Administrative Centre, though some do say that's a little presumptuous. Usually these are those of the Catholic persuasion.
DB: OK – Is that the place from which the Anglican Church is administered
AH: You could say that sir. Which department do you want?
DB: I don't know really. I'm in France and I just found a church
AH: I imagine that there are many of those in France Sir. I understand that most of them are of the Catholic Faith.
DB: No, No I am referring to the Anglican church
AH: Yes Sir the Anglican Church spreads its tentacles far and wide. The only true faith.
DB: No, no, you misunderstand. This is a real church, bricks and mortar, tower, no roof, big front door and so on
AH: You say this is made of brick, sir
DB: Well no, not really, it's a stone church. The tower has crenellations and a little flag sticking out of the top, and there's a roundy bit at one end..
AH: (Humouring me.) Well Sir I do know that many churches are made of stone – we have a large number on our books and...
DB: Listen, let me talk to someone in charge there. I'm a vicar

AH: A vicar you say, (aside to neighbour)– we have a right one here . This guy tells me he's a French vicar and he's found a church. Wants to speak to the boss – what should I do?

AH2: Oh Lord, one of those. Put him through to the Janitor –That'll sort him out.

AH: Hold on Sir I'm putting you through to another department

J: Hello sir, Janitor here, how can I help? Did you want your room cleaning?

DB: Who? No No, this must be a mistake I'm in France

J: My remit doesn't extend to France I'm afraid sir, Its all I can do keep the people in this building clean and tidy.

DB: No listen carefully. I'm a vicar living in France and I've found a church. I want to speak to somebody about it.

J: (humouring me again) I see sir. That's a very interesting story. And where would this church be?

DB: Well it's in a place called Vernet les Bains in the French Pyrennees, you know, Rudyard Kipling and all that.

J: I see. So are you Mr Kipling sir?

DB: No, No he's been dead for 80 years. Listen can I speak to someone who knows about these things.

J: What things would they be sir?

DB: Well lost churches in France I suppose.

J: Well sir we don't actually have a lost and found churches department here, This is an Anglican establishment. But I'll do my best. (Puts down phone)

Act 2 - 10 minutes later

DB: Hello hello is that Anglican headquarters

AH: (Oh God he's back again) It is sir, I take it that you are the (loon..) er vicar who just rang.

DB: Yes I am – the Janitor couldn't help. Please put me through to someone in authority.

AH: Well Sir they are all busy right now but if you could give me your email address I'll have them contact you through the net.

DB: I don't have an email address, I don't have my computer. It's at home in Pau.

AH: Well sir, in that case, I'm afraid that we can't be of help to you.

DB: Alright, I can tell that you think I'm three candles short of an altar but please believe me that this is a genuine call, I am a genuine vicar and the church is a reality in stone. I'm looking at it at this very moment.

AH: Well spotted sir. If you give me your name we can perhaps verify who you are and ring you back.

DB: My name is Blevin, I live in Pau and my parish was in Lesser Wittering by the Sea some years ago. My phone number is xxxxx

AH: Right Sir I'll look that up and let you know.

Act 3 - 2 days later

DB: Hello Hello, is that Anglican HQ.

(Different telephonist) Well Sir it depends on what you mean by HQ, this isn't a....

DB: I Know I know, a military establishment or a corporate business. It's God's administrative Centre. I rang two days ago and your colleague said that someone would ring me back. No-one has

AH: Which colleague would that be sir.

DB: I don't know he didn't give me a name. But I gave him mine. It's about a church I found in France.

AH: Ah I see (he's back again.) Well sir this is the Anglican Central Office. I can give you the number of the office of our Catholic brethren in Westminster if you wish.

DB: No, No don't do that. Let me repeat. My name is Blevins, I'm a retired vicar living in Pau and I have found a church in Vernet les Bains. An Anglican church. Please put me through to someone in authority.

AH: Alright sir, you can speak to the prebendary, he's the duty cleric at present

DB: Thank you very much. Maybe I'll get somewhere now

AH: Excuse me for disturbing you sir but I have a Mr Blevin on the phone. He says he has found a church,

P: Oh lord, one of those, Can't you deal with it?

AH: Well sir he's very insistent.

P: Oh well, I suppose I'll have to humour him. Put him through

Hello this is the prebendary speaking. How can I help you

DB: At last someone in charge. Listen I'm terribly sorry to bother you but I've found a church and I don't know what to do with it.

P: I see, a church you say, and you have some difficulty in doing something with it. Where is this church.

DB: It's in France, a place called Vernet les Bains. You know Princess Beatrice, Rudyard Kipling and all that.

P: OK Mr Kipling, Is Princess Beatrice there with you at this moment?

DB: No No, you've got it wrong. Kipling and Princess Beatrice have been dead for more than 80 years

P: I thought so sir, so why are you impersonating Rudyard Kipling, who I understand you to say has been dead for more than 80 years?

DB: I'm not! My name is Blevin. I'm a retired vicar from Pau

P: How do you spell Pau sir I'll look it up in the English church calendar.

DB. No No , Pau is in France I just happen to live there

P: I thought you said you live in Vernet les Bains

DB: No No I don't. I'm just visiting and I've found a church – an Anglican church.

P: I see sir and how you know it's a church and not a house built in the shape of a church

DB: Well it's in stone. And it has a tower with a flagpole sticking out of the top and big wide door.

P: Many houses have something similar sir.

DB: No No, listen, I've looked inside. It's got pews and an altar

P: Are you sure this isn't another Catholic church I understand that there are many of those in France. They also have pews and altars.

DB: No I'm sure it's an Anglican one. For a start it's called St Georges

P: Vernet is in Catalonia isn't it sir? I visited it once. I'm told that the patron saint of that catholic part of the world is also St George

DB: Yes he is, but the mayor has told me that it is Anglican and was built on a subscription organised by Princess Beatrice and Rudyard Kipling in 1913. I just found it again.

P: I see, like the 100th sheep it was lost and has been found.

DB: Indeed so. So what do you suggest I do with it.

P: Er well there are several possibilities, but let me look it up in the Anglican records and come back to you. You said that your name is Beatrice Kipling didn't you? I'll look you up too.

B: No No My name is Blevin, Donald Blevin; Round here they call me Blev the rev . My old Parish was in Lesser Wittering by the Sea . Ring me back quickly because I'll be leaving in a couple of days time. My mobile number is xxx

P: Well Mr Blevtherev, I will try but these things take time and first I have to find out where the records are – they could be anywhere.

DB: Thank you for believing me (puts phone down)

P: Believe him? Lost and found church indeed and in France. It's probably more a lost soul affected by the cheap wine. Which reminds me. After such a trying phone call I badly need a large drink of that lovely communion wine we bought last week.

Act 4 - 2 days later

DB: Hello hello is that Anglican HQ

AH: Well we are not......

DB: I know, I know - a military establishment or a corporate business. I rang 2 days ago. My name is Blevin. Can I speak to the prebendary.

AH: Which prebendary would you like to speak to sir

DB: I don't know he didn't give me a name – the one who was on duty on Wednesday

AH: Can I say what it is about sir.

DB: It's about a church I found in France.

AH: I see sir, and your name?

DB It's Blevin, Donald Blevin.

AH: Thank you sir. (looks up notes -reads 'on no account put this person through to me again!') I'm afraid that the person you spoke to last time isn't there sir – is there anyone else you would like to speak to.

DB: I don't know – the bishop perhaps.

AH: I'm afraid that the bishop is at a convention in Brazil sir but I can put you through to his secretary.

DB: I'm not sure if that will help but at least it's a try.

AH: I'm sorry to put this loon on to you Doris, but he's so insistent. Can you humour him for a while.

Bishop's Secretary: OK, I'll speak to him in words of one syllable, like I do with the Bishop. Hello, I am Doris, the bishop's secretary . How can I help?

DB: You don't know how relieved I am to hear a female voice. Maybe I'll get some sense. My name is Donald Blevin, and I have found a church in France

BS: I'm sure Mr Blevin, that there are....

DB: Yes I know many churches in France and most of them Catholic, but this the third telephone call I have made and it's getting very expensive for a retired vicar.

BS: A retired vicar – what did you say your name was

DB: Donald Blevin and my Parish was Lesser Wittering by the Sea

BS: OK. So about this church. Who have you talked to before

BS: The Janitor and the duty prebendary last Wednesday.

BS: Janitor? That's strange. So why aren't you talking to him now?

DB: Because he wasn't able to help, being the janitor and all.

BS: So why not the prebendary?

DB: He promised to ring me back and didn't and I am told that he isn't there today.

BS: Just hold on a minute while call another line

Hello – I have this man about a lost church on the line.

P: He's a nutcase – says he's a vicar called Blevtherev – so I looked it up and there's no such name. And neither is there an Anglican church in a place called Vernet les Bains.

BS: I see, so I must humour him then.

P: Do what you think is right.

BS: Hello Mr Blevin, I understand that you have found a church. Does it have big windy spire on it?

DB: No it doesn't and please don't patronise me. Give me your mobile number and I'll send you a picture of it from where I'm standing.

BS: I don't give my mobile number to strangers but if it has email you can send it to Doris at anglican.com

DB: OK here goes

BS: Wait a minute while I switch my computer on (pause). It's a very pretty church. Why do you think it's Anglican?

DB: Because I now see that there is a notice outside it that says St Georges Anglican Church. It was built by subscription from Princess Beatrice and Rudyard Kipling.

BS: Well that sounds convincing. Can you ask those two people to give me a ring to confirm your story.

DB: No I cannot – they're dead, deceased, under the sod and have been for more than 80 years.

BS: Oh dear, that does create a problem. I should tell you that we have no record of a church in a place called Vernet-les Bains, but you could call the Bishop of Europe. He's somewhere in the Mediterranean sea. I'll give you the number right now .

DB: Listen, I'm leaving this place today and I can't afford any more long telephone calls . Can you ask him to ring me.

BS: Oh dear I don't think he would do that, but his secretary might. What's your number.

Act 5 2 days later in Pau

ES: Hello, I'm looking for a man called Blevthrev, Is that you?

DB: Yes and No. My name is Blevin and people call me Blevtherev because I'm a retired vicar.

ES: Oh that might explain why no-one has ever heard of you. Sounds pretty irreverent to me (Bm Bm) I'm the Bishop of Europe's secretary and I understand that you have found an Anglican church.

DB: Yes it's in Vernet les Bains - you know Kipling and Prince...- Oh forget that bit.

ES: That's very interesting. You should know that we lose churches all the time out here. Why only the other day someone called in – said he had found one in San Paulo – That's only 20 miles from here and we didn't know about it. Strange thing to lose I know but there you are.

DB: So you believe me then. Hallelujah. I know I'm a bit absent-minded, being an aging vicar, but I was beginning to think that I was looking at a mirage of a church in Vernet. You know that Kipling and Princess Beatrice organised the subscription in 1913?

ES: Didn't know the baking company had been going that long. Yes we believe you. You wouldn't credit the number of lost churches there are in Europe of which we know nothing. It's all very comforting to know that Anglicanism had such a wide reach.

DB: Yes it is - compared to these godless times. OK So what do you intend to do with it?

ES: What do you mean do with it?

DB: Well we can resurrect the Anglican Faith in the town. There are loads of Brits in the area and I'm sure we can get a decent congregation going. Only thing is, it's in a bad state of disrepair and needs money spending to bring it up to habitable standards.

ES: Oh dear. I'm afraid that we don't have any money for that sort of thing in Europe.

DB: Hm. That's disappointing. So where do you think we might get the money from?

ES: Well you could try the Archbishop of Canterbury in the UK, but I don't hold out much hope. He's always saying that he's stony broke. Best thing to do is to donate it to the local council for a small fee and hope that they'll do something to help.

DB: But they're all catholic round here. They're not going to fork out for an Anglican restoration.

ES: Well you could try the Anglican Headquarters in London but I doubt they'll do much.

DB: You're right. They'll tell me that this isn't a military establishment or a corporate business and pass it to the Janitor to pay. Thank you for your advice and, above all, thank you for believing me. I was thinking of sending for the men from the Alzheimers Unit. Can we count on the Bish to be present when we ordain a new chaplain?

ES: Not sure about that. He's got a big area to cover. But you never know. Bonne Chance

As you will have seen, my ministrations had fallen upon mostly stony ground. But I remembered the words of our Lord on the mount. Particularly blessed are the pure in heart, and blessed are the meek, for they shall inherit the earth. And believe me, though it may have been yet another deadly sin, it was the earth around that church that I was determined to inherit, by all means possible, for my new flock. So I extended my holiday, made a few decisions and sought to have an interview with monsieur le maire of Vernet les Bains.

Act 6 - 4 weeks later

DB: Thank you for seeing me M le Maire. You will know that your town contains one of the most significant heritage sights in Europe. I refer to St Georges Church near the Casino.

M: Hein? – Qu'est-ce qu'il dit? (What did he say)

Mayor's secretary : Il a dit que St Georges est une superbe exemple de la Patrimoine europeenne dans notre ville. (He said that St Georges is an excellent example of European heritage and it's in our town.

M: Aha. Qu'est-ce St Georges? (What's St Georges)

MS : C'est une eglise pres du casino. Construit par Rudyard Kipling. (It's a church near the casino constructed by Rudyard Kipling)

M : Ah Oui? Je n'ai jamais entendu. L'entreprise aurait ete liquid. (Never of it or him The company must have gone into liquidation). Il veut de l'argent comme tous les autres n'est-ce pas ? (He wants money like all the others doesn't he?)

DB: Yes M le maire, with a small matter of 120,000 euros it can be made into a superb working church for all the Anglican residents in the Conflent and beyond.

M: Combien il a dit? (How much did he say?)

MS : 120,000 euros M le maire.

 M : Ridicule. On pouvait achete le Bank d'Angleterre pour ca. Qu'est qu'il y a pour nous dans cette affaire. (Ridiculous , we could buy the Bank of England for that. What's in it for us?)

DB: Ah yes M le maire, I was coming to that. We propose to make it available as an exhibition and leisure centre for the town during the week when we don't need it.

M: Qu'est-ce qu'il a dit?

MS : Il a dit, m le maire. que l'eglise est un beau centre d'exposition (He said the church would make a good exhibition centre.

M : Nous en avons déjà. Qu-est-ce qu'il y a d'autre pour nous. (we have one already, What else is in it for us.)

DB: I was coming to that too. As a sign of our goodwill we propose to donate the whole building to the town for a small fee.

M: Qu'est-ce qu'il a dit.

MS : Il veut nous donner l'eglise pour une petite quelque chose (He wants to give us the whole building for a little something)

M: Combien (how much?)

DB: 1 euro

MS: 1 euro?

M : Incroyable. Nous pouvons presque afforder 1 euro. (Unbelievable - we can almost afford 1 euro)

DB: But of course you would be responsible for bringing the church up to exhibition and worshipping standard

M : Qu'est-ce qu'il a dit.

MS : Nous serions les responsables pour sa restoration. (We would be responsible for restoring it.)

M: Ah! Mais ca nous apartiennerait? (but we would own it?)

(aside - if its ours we can do what we want)

DB: And there are many heritage associations in France who would donate funds to pay for that restoration.

M : Qu'est-ce qu'il a dit?

MS : Il a dit que nous pouvons utiliser les fonds des association patrimoines. (he said we can use heritage funds)

M: Ah, maintenant vous parlez. .(Now you're talking)

DB: And we would undertake to pay 20,000 euros as a sign of our goodwill

M: 20,000 euros? C'est une affaire–(its a deal). (Aside - that should pay for my new patio)

And so the dirty deed was done. A contract agreeing the responsibilities of each partner was drawn up. St Georges Anglican church in Vernet les Bains in the French Pyrennees would be sold to the town for 1 euro and the town council would apply for funding to the various heritage associations who have money for restoring heritage buildings. We, for our part, would hand over 20,000 of our precious loot and advise as the project progressed. The lost church had been found and disposed of. Now the small matter of raising a congregation with a vicar (me) who lives a 5 hours drive away in Pau and a scattered community of Brits, some of whom, I knew not which, were practising Anglicans. So, as is the way of these things, I called a meeting, and those who were present formed the committee, chairperson (me again), treasurer, secretary, churchwardens, sidespeople, gravedigger etc and we went to work. All of this on the basis that no-one would need to fork out a penny for church restoration. Over the next two years, the congregation grew slowly, rather too slowly for my taste, though probably faster than that at Lesser Wittering. Services were held on every other Sunday when I would risk life and limb, and that of the other drivers, on the French Motorways in order to administer the offices in temporary accommodation near the town square. One of our more fashionable events was the Christmas service – the brits round here love a bawl- when, each year, we managed to fill one of the local, unfortunately catholic (St Georges still being open to the elements), churches to over-flowing with sounds never heard this side of the Styx. The liturgy of 7 lessons and carols proved to be a popular show with the locals, French and British alike. I was never sure of any real commitment to the greater glory of God among the congregation at these occasions, but there was always the chance of a Damascene-like conversion.

Thus, progress was made on all English fronts but then, in the 2008 municipal elections, the composition of town council took on a harder, less cooperative, edge. The town was put under restriction for over-spending its budget. The years passed by with nothing done to carry out its part of the bargain. It was like dancing with a three-toed sloth – sluggish forward movement followed by an about-turn which brought us back to the point of departure. After a few futile attempts to appeal to the better instincts of the new Vernet Council, I was convinced that the blighters had never intended to fulfil their hallowed obligations. It was at that time that I decided to reduce the stress and retire definitively. No-one was interested in my long, carefully drafted sermons, and the battle to restore the glory of St George of Vernet les Bains was increasingly frustrated by the dragon of French indifference. It was affecting my health, which has never been good since I moved into the Parish Manse of Lesser Wittering by the Sea.

Luckily for me and for the church I had succoured into life, another ex-Vicar moved into the area and willingly took on the labour of love, preferring it to the head-banging oblivion of French television. Though his French is as good, or rather as non-existent, as mine, he's a much younger chap with a constitution and energy to match. Unlike mine, which has been church-centred throughout my life since Higher Education, his background is from the university of life. Cruel fate caused him to be born in Yorkshire, but I am sure that the gentle life of la France Profonde, and dedicated adherence to the task of marketing the true faith in an environment populated by so many of the opposition, will take away those harder edges.

I hear that last month there was some good news. Progress has been made. The heritage fund has coughed up a goodly sum, the Mayor is onside and will seek additional funding, and the holy work is promised to start in September, though experience tells me that the year, not having been specified, has also yet to be agreed.

So that's my story. I merely continued what had been started almost a hundred years ago. No, let me rephrase that - what had been started 2000 years ago. Returning the 100th sheep to the fold. Disappointingly, the fold is old and rickety, and since then many more sheep have escaped its warm embrace. But returning them is a job for those much younger than I, and for those as yet unborn. I pray every night that they will be successful, but fear that the embrace of Mammon will be too seductive. Here endeth the sermon.

Postscript

At one point, wondering how I had become so gullible as to write this piece, I asked the chap who commissioned it to become a member of my new congregation – the ymmygrant I believe he calls himself in another part of the book, how pretentious can one get! Any way it turns out he's one those damned (in every way) dissenters. He said that Kipling was one too, both in thought and occasionally in word. Says he was brought up in the Unitarian church, whatever that means. So I asked him – he says the meaning lies in the word Unitarian, as opposed to Trinitarian. Didn't the blighter ever hear of the decision of the Council of Nycaea in 425AD? The second council, not the first in 415 – that's when they got it all wrong, before the Emperor Constantine asked the bishops to change their minds. The Nicene creed has been the bee's knees ever since. I could have delivered a 3 hour sermon on that if I were back in Lesser Wittering by the sea. That would have got them rocking in the aisles!

The Conflent Tales

Chapter the seventeenth

The Window Cleaners' Tales

or The Refenestration of Prades

Being the murky tale of Britain's Role in the Continued Spotlessness of Prades Windows

The Window Cleaners' Tales

As I think the immigrant said in the first chapter, the Canigou seems to have a multiplier effect on the number and orientation of windows in the town. Every house has to have a view of the mountain's majesty, the better that it might be worshipped. It is, after all, the sacred mountain of the Catalans. Many of the houses in Prades are three and four storeys high, a window-cleaner's worst nightmare, George Formby may have 'climbed that blinking ladder till he got right to the top',{ in order to see the 'newly weds at number nine (the bridegroom he is doing fine, I'd rather have his job than mine, when I'm cleaning windows', for those unfamiliar with Lancashire humour), but the effort it would take to do the same in Prades would probably diminish even George's ardour. And so, in the spirit of demonstrating how British pluck and determination has accepted the daunting challenge of Pradean windows, this chapter relates the story of four of the town's window-cleaning heroes, who they are, what they did and why they did it.

Paul is British window cleaner number 3 in Prades. He washed, rinsed and squeegeed the day long, always with an enigmatic smile on his face, as if to say 'What the hell am I doing here?' There is a good reason for this puzzlement. In an earlier life he was a high-level and successful businessman running a busy UK technology company with a South African partner. Their products were popular in Britain and abroad and the company was highly profitable. As Managing Directors the income was enough to generate a large 6 bed-roomed house (one room for the maid) and a comfortable, if overworked, lifestyle. All Paul's considerable life savings were invested in the company that bore his name. Life was good, the fruits of his labour greatly profitable. One week in 1994, he turned up at the office as usual to find the partner absent and, atypically, not contactable on his telephone. He shrugged it off as a temporary aberration. Maybe he was ill, or held up by traffic or in someone's bed. The same thing happened on the next two days. Paul became worried. A telephone call to the bank confirmed his worst fears. The partner was gone as was all the company money. Desperate efforts to recover it were made through the courts and Paul won his case. But actually finding the money, and the partner, turned out to be a different story. Paul was cleaned out, not only by the loss of his company and his money, but also by the legal bills for his expensive lawyers. At that point he sold his large house to clear the debts and came to France, where property was much cheaper and Britain far away, with his wife, Berthe and his memories of what might have been.

Hence the window cleaning, both to earn money and to regain his self-respect. A conversation with Paul is revealing. Outwardly he is a smiling and carefree character, but one can always sense the smouldering volcano that lies below the skin. He has been robbed of his future and it hurts badly. That said, the physical activity of transforming grime-encrusted shop windows into prime examples of translucent luminosity, usually acted as a catharsis for his anger. But there were days when it spilled out. When he could be seen attacking the Pradean vitrines with an expression of concentrated venom was the day to play the Pharisee and pass by on the other side. You were as likely to get an earful of embittered invective as a bonjour. Such outbursts were rare and became rarer as time passed. He was courteous to his customers and tried to expand the business, since there are far more windows in Prades than there are professional men to clean them. A French partner would be ideal but, quite naturally, there are a few thousand reasons why that is not a viable option for him. The alternative, then, was to take on a French apprentice from the hundreds of unemployed youngsters in the region of Prades. Give them a step up the ladder so to speak.

He signed up to do his bit for reducing the *chomage*. Alas, in *le Prade profond*, nothing is quite so simple as it seems. The Conflent, indeed France as a whole, is not a place that encourages the entrepreneurial spirit. For starters, companies taking on workers have to pay their salaries and then almost as much again in their social charges to organisations with such unlikely acronyms as the CSG, the CSG+RDS, CFP, IRCEM. AGFF, URSSAF, ASSEDIC, all of them bureaucracies of the state, complete with *fonctionnaires* whose task it is to make sure that each tranche of money is received on time and is allocated to the right national pot. That is just the *amuse gueule*. Add to it an *hors d'oeuvres* of contributions for pensions (two types, two charges), a side-dish of paternity/maternity leave, a main course of sickness leave, a dessert of holiday entitlement and dozen other eventualities for the chocolates, and the state's monetary gluttony is almost complete. Except of course for the bureaucracy. Paul's letterbox was liberally inundated with weekly forms to fill, and invoices from a whole variety show of other French state organisations with strange acronyms he hadn't ever heard of – CIPAV, UPS, CPAM, FNAL, CSA and the like. The bureaucracy was overpowering. It seemed that every French *fonctionnaire* had his hands around Paul's neck, trying to squeeze another social contribution, another drop of fiscal blood from his income.

But the straw that broke the entrepreneur's back for Paul was the attitude of the youngsters he employed. They turned up for work only if they felt like it. Another hour in bed in the morning only meant a few fewer windows cleaned. Where's the problem? Work, it seemed, was a pain for them – it showed in their every wipe of the cloth, every dip of the sponge, every step up the ladder. Nevertheless, turn up or stay in bed, Paul had to pay the charges, until that is he tried to opt out of the system. More aggravation from the French employment laws which banned the sacking of young workers in the first two years of their apprenticeship, and entitled every employee to severance pay from the previous employer. At this point Paul threw in the towel. He now lives in impecunious semi-retirement, his efforts to improve the French, and his own, economy having failed to jump the hurdles of state obstruction and youth indifference.

Paul wasn't the first Brit to splash water on French Windows. In fact, he is the third to take over the Prades window cleaning business. It was founded, 26 years ago, by a charming and loquacious Welshman, Owen, who crossed the channel on June the sixth 1944 with the Normandy Landings, was lucky enough to miss the bullets and met Monette, his Mademoiselle from Armentieres, while pushing back the Reichswehr. He hasn't revealed how he accomplished the treble, but it has certainly turned out to be a very harmonious and successful anglo-french union. After the war, he took his bride back to Britain to produce, raise and condition their nuclear family and to provide them with the luxury of dual passports. But la belle France was forever calling both of them and, more than 40 years ago, Owen and Monette came in their middle years to settle in Prades, where Monette became the district midwife for the town. However, Owen was not one to stay at home washing the pots and hoovering the lounge. Very few ex-army NCOs are. So he looked around for a nice little earner to supplement his army pension and to pass the time away. Wandering around Prades one day it struck him that the town contained an indecently large number of windows, and moreover, that many of them were not the cleanest in Europe. Forty years of passing traffic fumes before the by-pass was built had seen to that. He made some enquiries and found, to his great surprise, that no window cleaning business had ever existed in Prades. That was his Eureka moment. Restoring the windows of Prades to their pristine shining glory became his metier and his mission. Let there be light in residences and shops, and there *was* Owen. For the succeeding 15 years Owen mopped and wiped and bucketed his way along the route nationale and the town square until compulsory retirement forced him literally to throw in the sponge. He has many tales to tell of those days and he willingly tells them to anyone who will hear. Of the time he was summoned to Eus to clean the exterior windows of Boris Vian's widow, Ursula. On arrival he found that one side of the house was built on top of a cliff. Not having a ladder 75 feet high he improvised a sponge on a long stick and did the job from the top down. Or the woman who made off with his bucket while he was on top of the ladder drying a third storey window. He never saw the bucket again. Or again the interminable exhortations to reduce his charges by clients unused to paying to have their windows cleaned by a professional. And not to mention the number of times the cheque was in the post......

Entrepreneurism and the application of new decor obviously runs in Owen's family. His son, David, followed them out to Prades, and he now brightens up the interiors of the local houses through his successful painting and decorating company, while Sophie, his daughter runs the *Bureau de Tourisme* in Prades with a terrible efficiency. Equally proficient in fast French and furious English she organises events for the town that it had never thought of before. Carnivals, International days, intercultural societies, Christmas markets and more - all alien ideas before Sophie's boundless energy made them possible. Her husband, Frank, has also joined in the capitalist spirit by establishing a landscape gardening business and winning the contract to beautify the region's open spaces. Regretfully, tempus is forever fugitting to the Murphy's Law of Fate, as Paul will testify. Fifteen years ago, Monette, one of the most energetic and vivacious of ladies in her prime, contracted Parkinson's disease. Her health has deteriorated to the point where she has to be in a home, while Owen, now in his late-eighties, is an increasingly frail version of his former window-cleaning self. Nevertheless , one last twist can be given to this story. Although Monette sadly passed away some two years ago, this year Owen was presented with the Legion D'Honneur, France's top military honour, at a ceremony carried out in the Prades square. This was for his part in the liberation of France and his service to the 'ancien combattants' the former soldiers of the Conflent region, and not his care and attention for the windows of Prades. A French General, the local military band (mostly the dance band and anyone who could blow a trumpet, recruited for the occasion) performed the ceremony watched by his family, all the local brits and a goodly number of French. How Monette would have loved to see this. Why this happened so late in his life is explained by the fact that the honour has to be requested, and no one had thought to do so, until last year.

Between Owen and Paul as launderers of Pradean windows came Bill, formerly a Public Relations director with a major multi-national company. The circumstances of this apparently massive demotion are not at all suspicious. Having taken early retirement, and arrived in the Conflentais Paradise at a youngish age, and having no skills that the region could, or would, use, Bill simply thought that it would be a good wheeze to clean windows for a few years. Only a Brit could think, and act, in that way. Moreover this was for him more a promotion – from doing something of doubtful value to humanity to doing something that benefited the community. And so, for 5 happy years he brought illumination and enlightenment to the good burgers of Prades. Since money was not his primary purpose, this worked well for debtors and creditors alike.

To visit Bill and his wife Joan, a former teacher of German, is an adventure of Odyssean proportions. They live in their eyrie of *Nohèdes* up in the clouds beyond the village of Ria. If we thought many roads in this area twisted, this one seemed to gyrate. It is the Scylla and Charybdis of the local transport system. Further it was horribly narrow with more blind spots than the one-eyed Cyclops rising from 1000 fathoms. We wondered how Bill had made this 20 km journey every morning and every evening for 5 years and remained alive. Luckily there was little traffic, as with all the minor roads in this area. When driving on them one can be forgiven for thinking that the bomb has dropped without your noticing it. The road climbed, under cliffs, round hairpins, through half-ruined villages, past vertiginous unprotected precipices overlooking the valley below until the Bill and Joan Berchtesgaden comes into view. And what a siren view! One can imagine the sirens luring unwary drivers over the edge. To be certain it is best to follow the example of Odysseus and, in the absence of a ship, to strap the driver to the steering wheel and to fill the passengers ears with wax to avoid being sucked into the seductive vortex of such colour and beauty.

Nohèdes is a beautiful place when it isn't raining, which happens with disconcerting frequency. Mountain trails lead onwards and upwards into the wild yonder and a nature reserve centre graces the annexe of its *Mairie*. Here in the middle of this dramatic scenery, one has the impression that neither time nor humanity no longer matter. The small, voluntarily-maintained nature museum attracts the visitors and explains the geology, flora and fauna of the countryside.

As hosts Bill and Joan are certainly the gentlest of eagles and have a fascinatingly dispositioned house complete with bread oven, perched precipitously over the void.. While their house seems to hang over a deep valley, the patch of earth they call a garden is situated even closer to the abyss, on a tiny shoulder of land on the other side of the road. It is a true hanging garden, more vertiginous even than those of Babylon. Here they have built a swimming pool one side of which peers perilously over a 1000 foot drop. It is as well to keep your wits about you when swimming here, since climbing out of it on the wrong side could quickly give a new meaning to the phrase 'infinity pool'.

In the hanging garden, Bill has constructed a barbecue, though this is a poor word to describe the flamboyant gothic cathedral to the omniscient God of Singed Flesh which greets the admiring gaze. If the Committee of the Beaux-Arts, sitting in their academic eyrie in Paris ever get to hear of this imposing masterpiece, they will immediately slap a grade one listed building order on it. It stands like a mighty organ, complete with pipes, whistles and orifices. One doesn't barbecue, one venerates. Visitors are invited to worship before this flaming volcano of flues and chimneys, vents and apertures. They gaze in speechless homage at the wondrous altar, pork chops their hymn books, grilled sausages their spicy orders of devotion, while the sacrificial, flesh-purifying flames rise higher and higher, into and out of its burning jaws. Every meal is a mighty, joyful, requiem grill for the dead, in this case the dead pig, chicken or lamb. The breaking of the bread accompanies its Gloria, the cutting of the chop its Te Deum, and the Lacrimosa comprises innumerable litres of red wine swilled energetically into awe-filled stomachs. All the while, the smoking machine fills the air and consummates the occasion with a crackling, intricate cacophone of contemporary sacred music. It is idolatrous veneration at its most enjoyable, well-nourished prayers soaring upwards in search of the Ultimate Griddle.

Finally, replete with food, memories and stimulating conversation, the visitors will bid their generous hosts goodbye and retreat down the mountain like Moses after receiving the tablets to plan and build their own, somewhat less magnificent monument.

But now, in keeping with the tendency of the world to move on, we have the present incumbent - window cleaner number four. Guess what – he's a Brit, Well almost – he is from Yorkshire but we will forgive him for that, being one of the more educated ones. Brian bought the company from Paul a couple of years ago with dreams of becoming rich, and has regretted it ever since. He came totally unprepared for the physical and mental anguish of French small company life. Luckily his wife Doreen is a dab hand at book-keeping and they get by, even to the luxury of establishing a cattery at the end of their garden. Neighbours are treated to the seductive purrs and mews of myriad cats and kittens and the occasional squeal when one of them takes a dislike to another. They have not yet formed themselves into a midnight choir, such as Grimethorpe describes in a previous tale, but when they do, that will probably be the end of that venture.

Of such stuff are the British window-cleaners of Prades made, and as a bonus, the good burgers of the town can now enjoy the unfamiliar view of the outside from the inside. One wonders whether, in a hundred years time, the 27th generation of immigrant cleaners from the North will still be carrying their buckets and leathers up wooden ladders in the Conflent's capital city.

THE CONFLENT TALES

Chapter the Eyghteenth

Le Golfer's Tale

Being the tale of the madness that is golf in France and the trials of those who would aspire to birdie every hole.

Le Golf

OK so my name is Jacques and I play golf. My wife is Marie and she plays golf too, though not as often as me. You have no idea what passions those sentences provoke in a French breast. In many aspects of life, my countrymen are either violently for or violently against, be it politics, big business, religion or choosing a pair of shoes. Golf is no exception. Take my good friends Jean-Pierre and Rosamunde who used to live in French Africa where J-P had a veterinary practice. They now live in Prades with assorted sons, daughters and grandchildren - a dysfunctional, extended family with problems extending beyond the limits of what they would wish and can bear. But they are wonderful people. Many is the time I and my wife have enjoyed their vibrant, thoughtful and civilised company in the local restaurants, in our homes, on *randonnees* in the mountains. They have a wonderful sense of humour and a great intelligence. We meet together every now and then to play bridge with Paul and Virginie, an English French combination also of dry humour and intelligence, and two of our greatest friends here. Jean-Pierre is an excellent bridge player, a sort of French Eli, who can squeeze, double-dummy and end-play with the best, while the rest of us, who are at best rusty and at worst incompetent, act as foils for his subtle genius. They are among the gentlest and most helpful persons we have met here in the Conflent. Dr Jekyll would have strongly approved. That is until they cross the line onto the sports field. Then the French equivalent of Mr Hyde takes over.

Jean-Pierre's passion used to be tennis. He would go along twice a week to the veterans' tennis mornings and try his best to win absolutely every point, every failure to do so being a *catastrophe*, a *désastre* or sheer *désolation*. That was the limit of his blasphemy, but as he grew older and slower around the court, the disaster count mounted and the catastrophes became more frequent. And so, one morning after a cataclysm of failed smashes, net shots and double faults, he gave up the game completely and returned to being Mr Nice.

It wasn't to last long. Both he and Rosamunde found a new passion - *le golf.* – and threw into it all the fanatical fervour of a born again Christian and a re-energized suicide bomber combined. It didn't help that their son Jean, a natural athlete, took up golf one fine day in 1992 and in one year became a scratch player. For non-golfing readers, this means that he can give us average players a shot on every hole and still beat us. Jean is now a professional golfer and a fine teacher, but such is the lack of interest in golf here, and one suspects so entrenched is the system of patronage, he has difficulty in finding a job.

It is Jean who taught Marie, my wife, the rudiments of the game and thereby doubled our household green fees in one hour. He has also taught his own parents to play, such that *Le golf* has now taken over their lives and most of their waking thoughts. Speak to Jean-Pierre about *les greens, le five iron and le slice* and the light of fanaticism comes into his eyes. He is mentally with *son drive* at the 15th in Perelada last week, or the delicate chip over *le bunker* at the 6th in Falgos.

Paul is also a golfer and, after two heart attacks, Virginie looks after him with a superabundance of tender loving care. She is his wife, his nurse, his cook but, most importantly, his caddie. We usually play, the six of us, at courses in neighbouring Spain where the greens are huge and, in theory at least, unmissable. The practice of course is vastly different. They are also beautifully maintained and we can play all the year round. This would be a golfer's idyll were it not for the nuisance of having to spend an hour and a half getting there and an equally long time returning. One of our favourite courses, the Domaine de Falgos is 3000 feet up in the mountains, and a delight to behold. It is only just in France on the other side of the Canigou mountain from our home in the Conflent. The views are stupendous from every tee, the natural history acts as spectator to every shot and if the golf is forgettable, as it ever more often seems to be, at least we've had a great day out. Just to visit this course would instantly cause a damascene-type conversion for those of the Mark Twain 'golf-is-a-waste-of-a-good-walk' persuasion, and they would immediately seek out the nearest pro-shop for a half-set of the best Taylor-Mades.

Up hillsides it winds and over ravines it soars. It is not a course for the faint-hearted, the vertigo-prone or any golfer with a questionable heart condition, Paul excepting. Nor is it a course for those, like me, who massacre the ball 260 metres (remember, this *is* at 3000 feet) in every direction except 12 o clock. It is as well to stock up plentifully on old balls, especially when the *tramontane,* our local version of the *mistral,* is blowing. The wayward shot is cruelly punished with the purgatory of a 60 degree ascent or descent amid infinite acres of acicular gorse, and with little prospect of finding the tiny white sphere. Half a dozen others maybe, but not one's own.

From the ninth tee, right at the top of the course, the majesty of the Canigou, 20 kilometres away, waits for the long hitter to blast the ball over the mountain top, and such is the descent of the slope, that even a raw beginner achieves 200 metres for exceeding the end of the tee. There are holes for those who slice and for those who hook - there is even a hole, the 12th, for the golfer who can do both in one shot. The last two holes ascend, almost perpendicularly it seems, from the lowest point of the course onto the huge plateau green below the clubhouse. It is there, within sight of sweet salvation, that cardiac fitness has its most testing examination, and is occasionally found wanting.

The last time we played here was in a friendly competition with the McPhersons, local Scottish friends who had been celebrating their 30th wedding anniversary. The extended family was there for the whole weekend and had lived it up as only the Scots can do on these occasions. At precisely ten o clock on the Monday morning, not a good time to play golf at the best of times, but doubly unsound after a weekend of solid carousing, Douglas stood proudly, or rather swayed precariously, on the first tee. After 3 swings his club and the ball had not made any sort of contact, but being golfers and gentlemen, we allowed him to use these as practice swings. Fourteen holes, seventeen balls, a thousand gaelic oaths and one blinding headache later Douglas, who normally plays off a handicap of 12, conceded the match and staggered off the course, a broken man. Such is the effect of Falgos.

But the magnificently built red sandstone mansion which acts as a clubhouse, a hotel and a mountain holiday centre, is never far from view. Whoever came to this wilderness fifteen years ago and said 'Here lies a golf course', must have been the greatest visionary since St Augustine. But 5 million pounds, innumerable environmental discussions, and several tons of grass seed later, there it is, resplendent in its isolation and unknown to anyone outside the tiny local golfing fraternity - a millionaire's dream and his playground. The tragedy is that only superb marketing skills will save it from oblivion. Jean-Pierre, Rosamonde, Paul, Marguerite and I have played it many times and on each occasion we have had the place to ourselves. Visiting golfers don't buy a green fee - they seem to buy the course for the day. Golf is not a game etched deep into the French national psyche and those who do play it build it around the other essential items of the day. At 12 o clock, wherever you are on the course, it is time for *le déjeuner* and players make their way to the hotel for lunch. Alternatively they will set up their gastronomic stall on the nearest convenient tee. Here they will eat their *foie gras* and *oeufs russes* and accompany it with abundant slurpings of red wine. Hunger and thirst assuaged, they resume from where they left off.

It is enough to turn the average British club secretary or golf-playing colonel a bright puce. Further, they hoop and holler and chatter incessantly, the art of conversation and demonstrating pleasure being more important than the need for concentration and the etiquette of silence. Every good shot is greeted with a bellow of self-congratulation and every bad one a wail of self-disgust. And if this were not enough, shots mysteriously disappear from scorecards come the reckoning time. It is all very different from the British way of golf, but it is all hugely enjoyable and enjoyed - as long as you are not on a crowded course surrounded by low-handicap golfers. It is not surprising then that French golf clubs are not like British ones - there are very few members, few competitions and few handicap changes.

There is another way in which French golf differs. All golfers in France have to be personally affiliated to the French National Golf Federation, which, for the unpaltry sum of about £60, will kindly insure them against anything they might do on a golf course, like kill their opponent with a mashie-niblick, brain damage a member of the 4-ball in front by driving early or have a heart attack by sinking a 30 foot putt. They are not a clubby race of people - but, when they get the golf bug, as our friends Jean-Pierre and Rosamonde, they will relate tales - of the shot which bounced into the hole off a cow; of the deliberate slice which went twice round a tree before landing on the green and of the drive in the rain when the club went 300 metres onto the green and the ball stayed where it was - with the best of any British golf-club bore. The story of the French golfer who, with a 3 shot lead on the last hole of the British Open, went paddling in the local burn instead, does not go down well in the bar of the local golf clubs in these parts. But we know it happened don't we, and somehow, where there is a Brit, it seems to surface more frequently.

Some 6 years ago I was astounded to find that a Scottish Investor wished to build an international 18 hole course here in our own backyard Conflent, on the hills near the village of Marcevol. The site is superb, incorporating a priory, a bergerie and several acres of vines. It would rival Falgos in the magnificence of its vistas, the severity of its undulations and the opportunities for small boys to make themselves rich on the reselling of mysteriously disappearing balls. The local Mayor was ecstatic in his support for the venture. He did, coincidentally own most of the land, The prospect of tourist-driven employment in an area of chronic *chomage* impelled the economic development officer of the *conseil regional* to add his voice to the clamour for the new course. A hotel and several fairway-side houses would blend unseen into the landscape and provide yet more work for the needy. This was to be the first step in the transformation of the area into a sportsman's paradise, the potential of income and an end to rural poverty. For a good many of the Brits it was joy unconfined. And all of this for free, - the money, millions of euros of it, would come from Bonnie Scotland as venture capital. What an enticing panorama lay ahead for the future.

They had reckoned without the resistance to change that is endemic in Northern Catalunya. Immediately a 'golf-over-my-dead-body' association was formed based on the priory of Marcevol and the residents of that village, most of whom live in Paris and other parts of France during the majority of the year. It was rapidly joined by the local ecologists, ramblers, professional anti-everythings, farmers, rednecks, backwoodsmen and the French McCarthyites who considered golf to be an un-French activity, detrimental to the moral fibre of Catalan youth. A whispering campaign started. Tales began to be circulated that the source of the money was British gunrunning and drug barons. Water, that highly emotional subject in these parts, would be frittered away in vast quantities for the dubious pastimes of rich Anglo-saxons, leaving none for the poor peasants in the towns and villages. Elected officials were threatened. All of this was nonsense of course. The same reaction had been seen in previous attempts to build a horse-riding centre, a country club and a cycling track in the region. In a place whose main modern source of income is tourism it is a bizarre, but popular, tactic. And so, after all the years, we await the first rumblings of the mechanical diggers and seed-layers. It will be a long wait!

But not all is gloom. Here in the Conflent we have actually formed a golfing society. At a hundred members, it allows us to negotiate special green-fee deals at many of the surrounding courses. For impecunious pensioned-off brits especially this is good news. Having no course of our own we tend to play 2 or 3 times a month, when funds, and a golfers quorum, allow. Long gone are Paul, Rosamunde and Jean-Pierre, the first to the great golf course in the sky and the others to a retirement home in nearby Prades. For those who remain, the existence of a golfing society allows us to take part in the seniors inter-club team competitions in the Languedoc-Roussillon Region, a haven of some 18 golf clubs stretching from the Pyrennees to the Rhone delta. The Marcevol team is mostly British. Despite our paucity of practice, more often than not our little band of British brothers comes out close to the top of the league, even winning it occasionally, much to the chagrin of the larger golf clubs, and notwithstanding the creative accountancy of some of their players on the course. Indeed for the past 2 years we did win the regional cup for players over 16 handicap. As Corporal Jones might have said 'They didn't like it up'em.' So there is only one way to deal with this embarrassment. The 'ditch Marcevol from the league' movement has its roots in the local posh 27 hole club at St Cyprien which many years ago hosted the French Open. It hasn't happened yet and we have some support at the negotiating table. And until it does our fragile and ageing Dad's golfing army will continue to show British golf at its inconsistent finest on the *terrains* of the Languedoc.

There are so many more golfing tales, oaths and misty days in the mountains to relate. We who are left follow our passion all the year round – sweating unhygienically in the 40 degree *canicules* of July and August and shivering pitiably in the fresh-frozen mornings of December and January when even a mishit ball travels 400 yards along the icy surface. Like Henry the Fifth's army we acquit ourselves with honour on the *parcours* of Nimes, Montpellier, Beziers, Carcassonne and anywhere where there is a battle to be fought, a birdie to be had, a double bogey to be avoided. We are wretched, magnificent, pathetic, splendid, sad, amazing, psychologically-damaged nomads with a disease for which there is no cure. Even the doctors cannot diagnose this illness. They are all up in the mountains playing golf.

THE CONFLENT TALES

Chapter the Twentyeth

The Driver's Tale

Being a tongue-in-cheek cautionary tale for those who would care to drive in the Conflent

NB This is a story intended to amuse rather than to educate or deter – 99.9% of people bring their cars to the Conflent and survive.

The Driver's Tale

Some references have been made in these tales to the violent world of driving in this lovely but lethal part of the world. It's all true. My name is Jim and I'm an Englishman living in the Conflent. I came as a neophyte into the crazy, irrational milieu of the catalan driver. But I have learned – and how!. I write these words in my bathroom with a cold flannel around my head, a hand that trembles with fear and a mind that is slowly slipping away. This is no accident of age or illness. I am, or was, a healthy, sporting, reasonable human being of 48 years of age, though my present features might bring to mind the later stages of Dorian Grey. And it's all connected to my extraordinary experiences on Conflent roads.

So these are my words of advice if you ever visit these parts – don't drive a car, don't cross a thoroughfare (pedestrian crossings are particularly vulnerable), don't ride a bicycle and don't assume that you are ever safe on the pavement from the lunatics who roam the area in search of another victim. Above all don't ever, ever, accept a lift from a local. I know that these counsels might restrict your mobility and hence your enjoyment of what this beautiful place has to offer but at least you will stand a better than even chance of returning to your home each night with all limbs intact and your sanity relatively unimpaired.

I will explain why. You see, I once had a car. I still have it. Like most cars in the region it boasts the scars of battle - scratches and dents gained while stationery in the supermarket parking lot, a missing side-view mirror from a Honda that seemed to want to occupy space on my side of the road and a shattered hub cap from a tractor with an appendage as wide as the road it was driving on. That driver knew something I didn't - that agricultural machinery is always a superior weapon over cars when it comes to single combat on the highway, and the farmer is always right.

I used to coast the highways and byways of Europe with a carefree air, whistling a happy tune the while. Driving was my pleasure and my recreation. And then I came to the Conflent. I can recall with terror my last nightmare journey as clearly as if it were this morning. It haunts my dreams and shivers my soul. It was from Mont-Louis to Prades. Mont Louis you will remember is the Vauban-constructed fort high in the hanging valley of the Cerdagne where the French paratroopers practice jumping at their regimental Headquarters. It was built to keep those sneaky Spaniards from sassying down the Têt valley to pillage Prades, rape its womenfolk and pinch things off the market stalls on Tuesdays. Desperate people! From here the road tumbles down the torrent stage of the Tet Valley from four thousand to nine hundred feet in just a few kilometres, adorned with hairpin bends, vertiginous views, narrow-laned villages hanging over dizzy drops and the most suicidal drivers to be seen outside of Cairo High Street. I joined the line of traffic making the same descent, completely unaware of the terrors to come. Life was good, the sun was shining as it does on most days in this demi-heaven and the world smiled benignly upon me. I looked into my rear-view mirror, and was puzzled, and not a little alarmed, to see the car behind making efforts to enter my exhaust pipe. It stayed there as if it had a magnetic attraction to my rear bumper. Nothing I could do, which wasn't much since we were in a long parade of similarly minded drivers, would budge it. So I thought no more about it and closed up to within 3 microns of the guy in front. As we came to the first blind bend a white van, moving in the same direction, hurtled past us all on the other side of the road like a cheetah with a serious bowel dysfunction. Any moving object unlucky enough to be climbing the other side of the carriageway round the bend would have meant instant oblivion for at least 4 of us. Luckily for him, me and the Renault stuck up my backside, there wasn't one. Maybe white van drivers have a sixth sense about these things.

The pace of forward motion increased to the permitted ninety kilometres per hour and then more, much more, as we all careered, seemingly stuck together, round the bends, through the villages and down the slope. Any attempt on my part to slow down would have been the equivalent of summary execution. The line of some 40 cars was like a downhill runaway caterpillar on speed, while, at every hairpin, there seemed to be a white van driver bent on meeting his maker along with those unfortunate enough to be alongside at the time his luck ran out. This frantic motorcade lasted for ten kilometres until it arrived at the level-crossing of the little yellow train, mentioned in other tales, and handily situated in the middle of a series of sportingly steep twists in the road. Here we were unlucky – the train was about to cross, the barriers fell and everyone had to stop or die. A scream of brakes, a loud crashing of bumpers in front and behind and a white van alongside on the opposite carriageway whose front wheels had a clear view of the bottom of the gorge a thousand feet below. Several crazy lunatics in front had beaten the stop by zig-zagging around the barriers. I now know why the car behind stuck so close – my brakes helped him to stop without denting his or my bumper. This knowledge did nothing to reassure me of the sanity of my fellow motorists and indeed the first stirrings of real fear came over me. It was as if I was a contestant in a motorists' dance of death, every other driver a grinning skeleton at the wheel, eager to welcome me into the ranks of the undead.

I took a deep breath just to confirm that I could and, the train having passed by after much waving of hands, we all resumed the foxtrot – slow slow, quick quick slow. Being a Brit, and therefore the leader who sets an example, my instinct was to plump for safety at a reasonable speed, say eighty-five kilometres an hour, and this is what I tried to do. Well, the others were having none of this – one by one they raced past me at the most dangerous corners, defying death by squeezing in front of me to avoid the upcoming vehicles. Many drivers had telephones to their ears as they passed and were conversing with elaborate hand-gestures with some unseen person – maybe their Funeral Director. This of course slowed the rate of progress even more as I braked to avoid their trailing end, so that subsequent overtaking drivers shouted loud abuse as they sped by and some even shook their fists. I was evidently not kamikaze enough for them. This fast-slow-fast journey – the foxtrot having given way to a quickstep - continued at a greater tempo through Fontpedrouse and the giant Jacuzzis at St Thomas until, half-way along the journey, we reached the right-angled bend at the sanatorium of Thues. And here was where the inevitable happened.

As I approached the turn, I was confronted by a Porsch – what else? - fast bearing down on me from the opposite direction on my side of the road, evidently trying to replicate the white van manoeuvre, but without the same element of luck. Time to think fast or perish. So I performed a neat rightward flip through the gate and into the grounds of the sanatorium. A split second later I heard the unmistakable grind of metal on metal behind me as the immovable object of the following car collided with the unstoppable force of its adversary – the approaching vehicle. It sounded like total annihilation of both cars and drivers. Of course there was no better place for an accident to happen than right outside a sanatorium where a good supply of nurses could be found, but that is scant consolation to a dying maniac. By some miracle no other cars were involved, most of the following pack having long ago passed me at great speed down the twisting, turning road behind. More happily no-one was killed, despite the high injury potential from the twisted wreckage at the side of the road. Not that this had the slightest effect on the following vehicles, which accelerated past the carnage as if it wasn't there. It was as if the smoking remains of the two crashed vehicles gave them an adrenalin rush. Perhaps they thought that the two up-ended cars were a novel form of modern sculpture.

So I ascertained that no-one was seriously harmed, left my name as a witness and crept slowly back into mainstream traffic, leaving the two drivers to argue about responsibility. By this time I had a blinding headache, my body was shivering with fear and my hands were slippery with sweat. So I sought the shelter of an enormous pantechnicon in front, and speed reduced to a gentle seventy kilometres an hour. Conductors of such vehicles brook very little argument and have the clout to enforce it. Not that that halted the attempted self-immolation of car and van drivers dashing past the big brute at every bend, but it at least offered me safe harbour from approaching free-thinkers with zero road sense. We eventually, after crawling through the village of Olette, speeding through Joncet and negotiating Serdinya's bends reached the long dual carriageway approaching Villefranche. We were on the relatively flat part of the road at the bottom of the valley. Here the boy racers really came into their own. I accelerated past the lorry at what I thought was a safe hundred and twenty kilometres an hour – fast by most standards and a good ten kilometres over the legal rate. Not so. Cars, their drivers frustrated by the slowness of the lorry, raced past me so fast that I thought that I had stopped. I was tempted to open the door to see if the car had broken down. The attempted hara-kiri continued through Villefranche and down to the outskirts of Prades and my home, Against all the odds ,and despite all the carnage and butchery in the daily war of the Têt valley, I had emerged terrified but triumphant, a broken man but alive to reflect on the madness. I garaged the car and that is where it has remained for the past 18 months. My conclusion is that Conflent motorists, if this is the correct term, obviously prefer martyrdom to rational behavior on the road. And this happens every day of the year summer and winter – it is one of life's miracles that there are any of us left to drive it.

Drivers in France are never required to retake a driving test at any age and driving licences last unto death without need for renewal. I understand that it is part of the French obsession with the rights of man. Thus we have blind, deaf and batty geriatrics in charge of potentially lethal instruments of death with the right to create carnage wherever they drive, and infant child racers with all the confidence of youth, but none of the ability to justify it, together with all the wannabe Lewis Hamiltons in between. Now you may notice just the teeniest hint of annoyance in my words. This would not be an inaccurate observation. I would love to wheel out my motorised vehicle once more and to explore this wonderful countryside but until half the driving population of the region has stopped self-sacrificing itself on the altar of velocity, it stays where it is.

So if you insist on bringing your vehicle to the Conflent I suggest that you take an advanced course, not in driving - that would be useless here - but in car avoidance techniques. Most Brits like to think that French drivers are mad. French Catalan drivers have a reputation for madness even among the French drivers. And, for the most part, they are absolutely right. Driving and remaining sane appear to be incompatible to the local driver. White van owners are particularly lethal and suicidal – and lucky. The presence of an overtaking vehicle on the other side of the carriageway is the norm rather than the exception.

The route nationale 116 runs from Perpignan to Andorra, with the Conflent at its centre. In winter it heaves with traffic rushing to be first onto the ski-slopes. The return journey is, as we have seen, performed as if they are still on the black slopes of the pistes. In summer carloads of grockels drive along it in huge numbers to sample the scenery and taste the wine. Often they drive as if they are doing both at the same time, indeed many are. And this on some of the twistiest, turniest, narrowest roads in the country, on which blind bends are the default option and slow lorries the only sure constant. It is all this which has inspired me to develop the new Longworth imperatives of Conflent driving, to be applied in the *Pyrenées-Orientales* only. They are on the next page and are quite simple.

	The Longworth rules of Catalan Driving
1	If you are behind another vehicle, overtake. This is a matter of honour. Following another vehicle is a stain on your (wo)manhood
2	Always wait until just before a bend before you overtake. This keeps oncoming traffic on its toes and maximises the surprise factor
3	Never brake until the very last minute. The insurance company will always make the other driver pay for rear bumper collisions.
4	Solid white lines are just broken ones where they have mistakenly forgotten to put the gaps. So, once more unto the breach, lads
5	If you have a passenger, engage him/her in animated conversation with lots of hand movements and eye contact. Do this while driving fast. Put him/her in the back seat for maximum effect.
6	Never signal your intention. In this way you keep the other drivers guessing as to which way you will go. If you do decide to signal always forget to turn the blinker off. This causes maximum confusion for minimum effort.
7	If you are female, you can do anything you want on the road. All mirrors, especially the rear-view mirror, are placed there so that you can ensure that your hair is straight and your mascara hasn't run.
8	The recommended gap between you and the car in front is three microns. If It has a foreign number plate it is 2 microns or less.
9	Ignore all speed limits. They are there to annoy you.
10	Overtake as if long lines of traffic are exactly the same length as a single car. If a car approaches from the opposite direction, swerve into line only at the last minute. Remember the other guy will always give way.
11	The shortest distance round a corner is straight across it. This maximises both petrol consumption and annoyance to other drivers.
12	On narrow roads, always drive at speed in the middle. Make way for cars approaching from the opposite direction just at the point where the front bumpers are about to meet. Extra points if the other car lands in the ditch. Blind bends are particularly interesting places for this rule and may require some speedy manoeuvring. Extra points for catching his rear view mirror
13	Better dead than cissy

Somehow thirteen seems to be an appropriate number.

Post script

I finally took the plunge. If you can't beat them, join them. I de-garaged the car, took a deep breath, and drove for a few months in the Conflent manner. In its own twisted way it was quite exhilarating. It didn't take long to get into the swing of things and drive like a demented maniac. In the first month I picked up 5 speeding tickets, four scratches and a dent in the rear offside door. In the second I had another three speeding tickets and a mangled rear bumper. On the positive side I had inflicted minor damage on at least eight other vehicles, one of them a brand new Mercedes sports, ditched three cyclists and put the fear of death into three pedestrians who happened to get in my way on a zebra crossing. But it was the tickets that niggled me. When I asked my neighbour how it was that I managed to pick up the tickets while French drivers seemed to avoid them, he nodded sagely and said that the first law of local motoring is to know where the cameras are. 'We owl know wear zey are 'idden' he said 'and we simply slow down at zat place. Only ze étrangers and ze 'oliday makers are ever coat unless it is by one of zose snaky gendarmes with ze speed gun. I myself have been coat like zat joust tree times.' So he gave me a map with the situation of all the speed traps in the Pyrennees-Orientales and told me how to regain some of the points.

This involves paying money to attend a 'naughty drivers' course held monthly in Perpignan and other larger cities. So I did. And very entertaining it was. My fellow class-mates, wicked boys and girls, were mostly French and were there for a variety of reasons – driving while asleep, murdering a passenger, knocking old ladies over on pedestrian crossings, causing multiple pile-ups, partying while driving on the public highway and so on. I jest of course, though I can't be sure. Drink driving was the most common transgression and speeding too many times like me came second in the album of crimes of those present. So the instructors told us about accident causes and statistics, the effects of alcohol on driving, accident black spots and how to have respect for other drivers and backed it up with their own motorist version of the Hammer house of horror videos. I half expected Peter Cushing and Christopher Lee to make an appearance out of the wreckage. All of this already well known to the participants, some of whom were on their fifth course. The style was a mixture of alcoholics anonymous and the catholic confessional, everyone expected to acknowledge their sins and promise to cleanse their souls and mend their ways according to the driver's catechism. All delivered too in fast furious French which, for an errant étranger like me, was something of a problem.

Still, all that mattered was attendance. There was no final exam to prove that the precepts of good driving had been well learned. No threats of capital punishment for recidivism. In this way I have regained four of my eight lost points and next year I can recover the other four by going through process again – all providing of course that, in the meantime, I can find where those damned speed cameras are and that no sneaky gendarme points a gun at me while I am driving like the locals. And that I am still alive!
Bonne route

THE CONFLENT TALES

Chapter the Twenty-fyrst

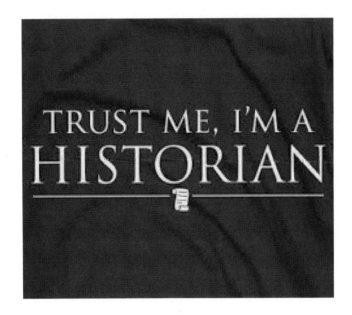

The Historian's Tale 1

The Retirada of 1939

Being the tale of a little known exodus from Spain into France at the end of the Spanish Civil War.

The Historian's Tale 1 – The Retirada of 1939

1939 was a difficult year for France. Not only did it experience the indignity of an invasion on its North East border from Hitler's hordes late in the year, the country suffered a very different incursion in its far South-West in the early months of the year. This latter wasn't a military attack, rather it resulted from the aftermath of the Spanish civil war, when a flood of desperate refugees from Southern Catalonia fleeing from Franco's bombs and reprisals knocked on the porous gates of the Conflent and its neighbouring regions in the Pyrenees-Orientales.

Despite initial French efforts to keep them out, almost half a million people crossed the French border over the Eastern Pyrennees in the depths of winter, suffering incredible hardships, hunger and deprivation on the way. The Gods of Winter didn't care to ease their burden. They provided one of the coldest on record. And so these ill-clothed exiles tramped their way in temperatures of minus 20 degrees up through the snow-filled cols and valleys. Along the coast they came, over the high mountains, along paths later followed in the opposite direction by the fallen airmen seeking refuge from occupied France. Along the 'route des aviateurs' (8000 ft) leading to Mantet in the Conflent, over the Coll d'Ares (5000 feet) to Prats de Mollo in the next valley, through the Cadi mountains (8000 feet) into the Kingdom of the Cerdagne and thence down the Tet valley to the Conflent. Families with children of all ages, grannies and granddads, exhausted soldiers and civilians, the poor, the destitute and the shattered – all hoping, expecting, that their cultural cousins across the border would recognize their plight and welcome them into their homes. Or at the very least offer them some kind of sanctuary.

Back in what was now Franco's Spain, many of the men had, for 3 years, fought bravely against the dictator's well-equipped forces, winning some battles, losing most. Side by side with them, the rag-tag army of the international brigades had made their own history, some of them retiring home to write about their experiences - Laurie Lee, Ernest Hemingway, Jack Jones, George Orwell and many others lesser known. But Franco had the support of the Fascist dictators, Hitler and Mussolini, and their massive contribution outweighed the occasional backing of the Soviet Union and the studied neutrality of other European nations. This, together with the constantly bickering factions in the Republican forces, made the difference between victory and defeat. More often than not, brute force overcomes naïve idealism and hopeful dreams., and when Barcelona became , the last Spanish city to fall on January 26th 1939, the cause was lost. Nor did Franco celebrate his victory gracefully. Determined to stamp out republicanism forever he blitzed the defeated army and its cities with the fervency of a born-again inquisitor. Debilitated by 3 years of unrelenting war and shell-shocked by the Franquiste bombardment hundreds of thousands of republicans, many with their families in tow, sought sanctuary in France. This was 'the Retirada,' the retreat.

But the refugees were no more welcome in France than Muslims are in America. The milk of human kindness seemed to have soured in the Pyrenees Orientales of the time. The France of 1939 was far from being the sister republic that would offer succour and support to its fellow Catalans. Enfeebled by an economic crisis, and in thrall to rampant xenophobia, similar to that existing in America, The UK and other European countries today, French society offered the refugees a less than enthusiastic reception. Maybe it was the indifference and disorder of a weak French government that produced this but I doubt it. Half a million is rather a lot of people for a small poverty-stricken department with no industry to take on board without preparation and support. After all, wasn't 25,000 the maximum number of Syrian refugees for the whole of France in 2015?

What to do with these intrusive fellow Catalans in the less sophisticated world of 1939? The answer was obvious. Declare them to be 'foreign undesirables' (a designation passed in the previous year by the national government) so that they could be legally imprisoned, and then put them into concentration camps - show those other invaders later in the year 1939 how it's done.

By the first week of March, 87,000 men alone had been incarcerated into what was euphemistically called an internment camp on the beach at Argeles-sur-mer. Here, enclosed by razorwire fences, they endured the ice-cold tramontane whistling down from the frozen mountains, the indignity of prison life and the kind attentions of Senegalese troops with a well-deserved reputation for ruthless violence. Nor was the cuisine of cordon bleu quality. After all cooking for 87000 by the seaside is a culinary and logistical challenge of Herculean magnitude. Even in modern times there are restaurants that haven't solved it. More often than not there was neither food nor water and what there was was barely edible At least in the later concentration camps there were shacks for the inmates and latrines, however primitive. Not here! No covered accommodation adorned the beach, not even a tent. The only place to sleep and defaecate was a hole in the sand. Dysentery and disease spread like a viral video and took their toll in lives - an estimated 17000 fewer mouths to feed in 5 months. Those who survived described how the favourite sport of some of the French guards was to beat up dying men. Dante could not have fashioned a more horrific scenario.

As for the women and children, they were better housed in the equally euphemistic 'accommodation centres.' At least most of them had a roof over their head and one meal a day. Scant recompense for losing both their dignity and their husbands due to circumstance.

Many of them were 'redistributed' to other parts of France with little chance of a future reunion.

The undoubted success of this neighbourly venture led the authorities to construct other rat-infested and squalid 'facilities' along the beach at St Cyprien and Barcares, slightly improved by leaky roofs and primitive shelter from the elements. The idea caught on even more with the arrival of the Nazis. Here was a whole new opportunity for inhuman conduct. A source of free labour, places for housing rounded up Jews, Gypsies and other undesirables before dispatching them to the death camps. Thousands of the exiled 'undesirables', having been on the wrong side of political orthodoxy, were exterminated in the Nazi gas chambers, mainly at Mauthausen in Austria. The majority, though, were conscripted into squads of foreign workers, unpaid of course, while others were sent to be further abused in the Foreign Legion. One of most notorious of these concentration camps, now immortalised as a museum, can be found at Rivesaltes, near to Perpignan airport. Never again it says on the blurb. Some hope! Here we are again in modern-day Europe and America behaving just as selfishly and mean-spiritedly in frantically denying sanctuary to the fallout from the world's battlefields.

And yet, and yet, as with all human endeavour there are beacons of honour and light. Most villages in the Conflent have several families with Spanish names. These were the lucky ones, who were taken into the homes of compassionate Catalans and whose descendants eventually settled down to make their own homes there. Although many returned to Spain, voluntarily or otherwise – often to suffer persecution, prison or death - others, in spite of their inhuman treatment, volunteered to join the French Resistance and contributed as "Guerilleros Espagnols" to the liberation of France in 1944. In March 1945 the exiles of the retirada were finally granted the official status of Political Refugees., six years too late. It is estimated that approximately a quarter of the Conflent's present-day population are descendants of these Spanish refugees, a positive testament to the healing power of time and longer-term planning.

Prades, capital of the Conflent, welcomed Pablo Casals, one of the world's greatest cellists as a resident, revered and accepted as an honorary Pradeen, To this day the Festival which bears his name, and takes place every year in July and August, is regarded as one of the foremost chamber music events in the musical world and it has spread its tentacles into more than 20 countries.

Casals vowed that he would never again play the cello while Franco stayed in power. He had a long wait. Franco stayed alive and in power in Spain until 1975, by which time many refugees had become French citizens or had emigrated to Mexico and South America. Many families were never re-united. Casals never realised his dream. He died in 1973, but he did play again and taught many young cellists who later became household names as soloists and players in orchestras around the world. The Festival gives Prades, a small town in the Conflent of no more than 6000 people, an international focus and an enduring legacy.

Thus ends this story of one of the major unsung human upheavals of the last century. Maybe there are lessons to be learned from the events of the Retirada for the present day. Or there again, maybe no one is listening. That would be more like human nature.

THE CONFLENT TALES

Chapter the Twenty-Second

The Historian's Tales - 2

Cathars and Castles

Chateau de Peyrepertuse

The Historian's tales - Cathars and Nazis

The Conflent is a place of mysteries. Many of our visitors comment that there is a magic about this place which cannot quite be explained in words. And they are right. It seems to have a supernatural aura about it. Perhaps the morning mist round the sacred mountain summit of the Canigou is really ectoplasm. Or perhaps it has something to do with the Cathars, who had their heyday nearby in the 12th century.

Cathars? Did I not mention those? No, they are not people with permanent nose-colds. The Conflent is not in Cathar France, since it was Spanish at the time but it was next door and was certainly a place of refuge for these unfortunate people in times of trouble.

For those who recognise this as historical witter, an explanation is called for. The Cathar religion flourished greatly in Southern France during the 12th and 13th centuries. It was a gentle cult, and for its time socially advanced, treating men and women as equals and drawing its priesthood, *parfaits* or *good men* as they were called, from all parts of the laity. Its philosophical and ethical credo came from the dualistic Gnostic and Manichaean traditions, banned from human contemplation several centuries before by the second Council of Nycaea. We historians like to show how clever we are by throwing in big words like that.

The world for them was an evil place, though they believed that good could be brought into it through righteous living. It persuaded by example and good living rather than intimidated with the threat of imminent hell. It considered the Catholic church to be morally and spiritually corrupt, which, at the time of the inquisition in this area had much basis in truth. The devotions and the consolamentum, perhaps the equivalent of catholic extreme unction, were carried out in the homes of people. Such a bottom-up people-focussed religion, a stark contrast to the top-down, believe us or we'll burn you approach of the dominant faith was, unsurprisingly, becoming so popular among the people of the area that it began to present a serious threat to the religious establishment. Not unpredictably, threatened with a visit to the local job centre, the bishops of the region petitioned the Pope to do something about this menace to their authority. The then Pope was in full agreement. He was having none of this challenge to his hegemony. Despite his name, Innocent III, he was not averse to a spot of gratuitous sadism nor was he well known for his tolerance of religious rights or any other rights for that matter. So he declared Catharism to be a heresy, in that inquisitional era as serious a fault as being a climate Scientist in the USA. He demanded that the then King of France, Philip the Good, who, like the Pope, hardly lived up to his name, should find a means of destroying the Cathars, preferably in an appropriately cruel fashion, '*pour désencourager les autres'*. In those days ruthless cruelty and brutality were the approved models for settling disputes and Philip found the perfect man for the job, Simon de Montfort, one of the catholic church's most zealous psychopaths.

It was a Polish philosopher who remarked on the arrogance of leaders - it was to the effect that those who consider themselves to be right 50% of the time are relatively normal, those who think they are 60% right may, or may not, be geniuses, those who could possibly believe that they are more than 65% right are suspect and should be on medication, those who decide that they are right more than 70% of the time are indubitably mad and should be put away, while the 80 percenters are the psychopaths and sociopaths whose delusions cause the greatest trouble.. Simon de Montfort was an out and out 100%er, much in the style of Stalin, Hitler, Osama bin Laden, Vlad the Impaler, Donald Trump and Thatcher, all of whom believed that they, and they alone had access to the final solution whether it be the gas chamber, the gulag, jihad or neoliberal economics. Simon's favoured methodology was burning. He knew with absolute certainty how people should behave and how they should be cleansed if they did not adhere to his simplistic view of right and wrong - not a million miles in outlook from the ISIL philosophy of beheading everyone who disagrees with them. Or the alternative facts doctrine that transforms truth into lies. Democracy did not come easily to him, not for him the ballot box, the reasoned argument or the pluralistic society.

For his task, De Montfort mounted an offensive known as the Albigensian crusade, so called after the town of Albi, a hotbed of happy Cathar dissent. His army of Northern knights were promised free land in the South if they did their derring well and efficiently. His philosophy, if that is what it could be called, was simple - recant or become carbon. All heretics must be burned and sent to hell, presumably for more heat treatment. And so he scorched and charbroiled his way through the towns and cities of the South showing pity to neither foe nor friend. Approaching the substantial city of Beziers, he ordered his soldiers to massacre the Cathars. When asked by one of his knights how they would distinguish them from the good catholics, his reply was typical of the tyrant with a personality disorder 'Slay them all, God will know his own.' This was Christian certitude at its best, every man. woman and child slaughtered in the name of God. Job done! Even Trump couldn't match that – yet. And so the bloodbath continued and De Montfort;s knights profited hugely. His army plundered, murdered and massacred its way throughout the towns and villages of the South of France. – Carcassonne, Montreal, Lezignan, Narbonne, amassing large tracts of Southern France for themselves in the process. The Geneva Convention not having yet been formulated, compassion, empathy, reasonable force was in short supply. Medieval torture proved to be an effective weapon of choice. It had the exquisite advantage of combining extreme cruelty with the building of a database of people for burning whether or not they were guilty. Trump, take note.

In this way, a large number of *parfaits* and brave ordinary people perished in the purifying flames of de Montfortian righteousness. But not before they had mounted a fierce resistance from their strongholds - what are now known as the *Châteaux de Vertiges*, of which there are many near to the Conflent. They are magnificent - what everyone believes medieval castles ought to look like, and in a place where castles ought to be - on the tops of the mountains for everyone to see. The Cathar *Château de Peyreperteuse*, about 30 kms away from the Conflent is still one of the most spectacular and evocative castles in Europe, if not the world. The view from its topmost keep would impress an eagle. It should be seen before dying and those visitors who suffer from vertigo will indeed probably die several times if they dare to explore it. The Chateau de Puilaurens is similar but different. The site may not be quite so vertiginous but the agony lies in mounting 300 metres up a seemingly vertical pathway to get there. But the views from the top are certainly a just reward for the effort. Standing there above the realm of mortal man makes one wonder how food and water enough for hundreds of hungry cathars ever made it to the mountaintop. De Montfort's brave men besieged these strongholds and starved their inhabitants into submission, only for them to be immolated below. Monuments to their fate can be seen at several places including Minerve in the Aude and at Montsegur, the last of the castles to fall in the Conflent's neighbouring department of the Ariege. All of these are in easy reach of the determined visitor to the region.

Puilaurens, Chateau de Vertige

Today of course such methods are frowned upon. We would much rather use nuclear rockets to annihilate those who disagree, waste them with chemical and biological persuaders and/or send drones to make them disappear. Torture is making a strong comeback as a persuasive tool of government to win hearts and minds, its techniques having been creatively enhanced by modern technology. The judas cradle has been replaced by chemical persuaders, the iron maiden by the innovative use of water and the head crusher by the tabloid press, equally effective at disengaging the brain. De Montfort would have been proud of his legacy.

THE CONFLENT TALES

Chapter the Twenty-Thyrd

The Lifelong Learner's tale

Being a rant about the need for learning and change even in the paradyse that is the Conflent and how it might come about.

The Lifelong Learner's Tale

You: OK. I've read so far. Highly entertaining and I enjoyed it. But a little bird tells me that you're going to start preaching . Is this where I shut off and close the book?

Me. Yes, of course, if that's what you want to do. That's your privilege at any point. But, honestly, all I wanted to do was to be a little more serious. And I'll try not to preach

You: Serious? You've got to be joking. Why do you want to go and spoil a good entertaining book like this?

Me: Hey - why can't it be entertaining and serious at the same time? When did you last laugh your socks off at a good thriller? And who says I'm going to switch off the entertainment. Tell you what. Bear with me for a few words while I try to make sense out of all this, and if you get bored you switch off. Is it a deal?

You : OK then, but don't you get too heavy. What's it about?

Me: It's all about Lifelong Learning regions. I bet you didn't know that Lifelong Learning is official government policy throughout Europe, Australia, Canada and much of Asia. Has been for more than 12 years.

You: No I didn't and for that matter, neither does anyone else I know. I don't even know what it is but sounds very educational and preachy.

Me: I suppose it is a bit, but learning's what you're doing all the time. After all - if you've read the book so far you know a hell of a sight more about the Conflent than you did before. And you must have been interested enough not to put it down. And you must be an intelligent learning person to have the book at all.

You: OK, If you put it that way, I might be, but I'm not admitting it. So what's the Lifelong bit?

Me: You know - cradle to grave, hatch to despatch, we had a bit of a brainstorm about it once and came up with a few phrases to describe a lifetime of learning. How about from maternity to eternity, from lust to dust, from sperm to worm, from birth to earth, from yearn to urn and from womb to tomb?

You: Hell, that's so corny I think I'm going to put this book down straight away.

Me: Sorry, just testing. Anyway, learning starts as soon as we're born – we're studying our parents and copying what they do, and pretty soon we can talk, walk, communicate, recognise pictures and give them the general run-around. That's a pretty impressive intellectual achievement for a baby. Huh?.

You: I suppose so, hadn't really thought about it that way.

Me: So now you're learning. We humans can't help it. We do it from day one – some say even before that, while we're in the womb. As I was saying, this Lifelong Learning gig is pretty important to us all, wherever we live and it's big.

You: Sez you! I haven't heard of it so it can't be that important.

Me: Like the blind man said - there has been an alarming increase in the things I don't see any more. I expect that Lifelong Learning has only received any publicity in the circles where you're not. The only reason you're reading it now is because it's here in this book - now. That's part of the problem. We're all bombarded with so much information nowadays - from tv, posters, radio, newspapers, the internet, mobile phones - that we can't always separate what's important or good or bad or indifferent from what's not - and sometimes you only receive from them what *they* think is important.

You: I've heard this one before. We're all being manipulated by the big boys and the press. So what's new. They talk and we listen - but nobody says I believe all I hear or read

Me: Nor should you

You: So why should I believe this?

Me: Clever! I told you you were intelligent. The answer is either no reason at all, or the thought that if you don't do it you'll never know what it would have been like if you had done it. But at least you could give me a hearing and judge it on its merits. To put it another way - I'll listen to all your unreasonable demands if you'll consider my unacceptable offer.

You: Sold! OK then, Press on - but not too heavy mind - You might exercise my brain too much. Anyway, is this Lifelong Learning business just a bee in your bonnet?

Me: Not really. I already said that Lifelong Learning is big policy, surprise, surprise - just about all the major world organisations - from UNESCO to International Corporations, OECD, most National Governments - are not only talking about it but they're also developing plans to do something about it by introducing Lifelong Learning within their spheres of influence. And if they're all doing it at least one of them *must* be right. Those are some other of the big boys you were talking about, but here's question for you. What did your grandfather do for a living?

You: What the hell has that to do with the price of fish?

Me: Go on indulge me.

You: OK he was a farm labourer. Does that explain why you're so high and mighty?

Me: Hey don't get all defensive. Mine wasn't much different, he was a cotton spinner. He walked the three miles to work every morning and home every evening because there was no other way to get there that he could afford. He did more or less the same job day after day for 40 years – doffing and cocking, changing and spinning. Guess how much learning he did for that job.

You: Pretty mechanical – a couple of days?

Me: That's about it – less in fact and all of it sitting with Nellie next door before they let him loose on his own spinning frame. And here's the rest of his history story. The din of the machines was so loud and continuous that he became a little deaf. So, during the first world war, like a lot of the others who wanted to escape from the grinding poverty of the cotton towns he joined up, and learned how to carry the dead and the wounded from the battlefields of Ypres and Paschendaele in Belgium. Not all learning is a happy experience.

Anyway, the shells screamed overhead and non-stop, the guns roared day and night, thousands died every week. For 2 years he was just a split-second from death. But he was one of the lucky ones – he survived -but none of that helped his deafness, or, on his return, improved his poverty.

You: Yeah, mine did something similar – he didn't have any formal learning after school, and he joined up too, but he never talked about what he did or so in the war. Kept as stum as a dead mole. So why are you telling me all this? It's a fascinating tale but what's the point?

Me: Bear with me, What did your dad do?

You: He used to read gas meters for the gas board – did that for 40 years. And before you ask he learned how to do it from his foreman in one day.

Me: Mine was unemployed for 6 years in the 1930s before he found a job as an insurance agent. Every day he would get on his bicycle and cycle from house to house, collecting the premiums from his customers over a territory of some 100 square miles, rain or shine, mostly the former. Bolton's like that. Like your Dad, he had one day's training

You: This is nice, swapping family stories but I'm getting bored. Tell me where we're going.

Me: Just one more question? What do all those people have in common?

You: Well, they were poor, and they didn't have much education for their jobs.

Me: Yep – you're spot on and here's one more thing. None of those jobs exist now. Now you and me we've been around a bit haven't we? We've had more than one job in our lifetime, even if we worked for the same firm, and every time we've had to get some training to do it.

You: Well I went to technical college for a year and I've done some retraining from time to time. That's true. Does that make me a lifelong learner?

Me: I suppose it does to a certain extent. But let's think what we want for our grandchildren.

You: I'd like mine to go to university and have the advantages that I never had. Maybe become a doctor or lawyer or an engineer.

Me: Me too – can you see what we're driving at – each generation is wanting to improve its chances and each one needs to get more and more education to do it. But there's more, much more to this story. Ever read any Government reports on future employment?

You: You gotta be joking. Why should I bore myself stupid with all that crap?

Me Well you just might learn something – and it sure affects your grandchildren and what they will do. What's your grand daughter's name?

You: Susie – but you knew that

Me: So I did , I asked just so the readers would know. How old?

You: She's 10, You knew that too.

Me: OK. She's likely to live until, let's say, 2080, at least. So what's the world going to be like then?

You: Haven't a clue – spaceships buzzing around the streets? Everybody with their own robot?

.

Me: You've been seeing too many Science Fiction films. I'll give you a clue – It's 2017 now OK? Some government boffin reckons that 2025 – that's when your granddaughter finds herself looking for a job if she goes to university, right? the jobs that will be available haven't yet been invented. We don't know what they're going to be.

You: That's government boffins for you. Head in the clouds, don't know their arse from their elbow.

Me: Maybe. We've seen a few changes in our lifetime haven't we?

You: How do you mean?

Me: Well when I was born in Bolton there were 300 cotton mills and 50 % of the people lived off the cotton industry. Now there's one, and that's under threat. There was no TV, No mobile phones, No cashpoints, most families didn't own a car, we had smogs, high mortality rates, we drank Vimto and every child seemed to thrive on licorice sticks.

You: Yes I remember. We played out in the street, used lamp posts for wickets, coats for goalposts, went to Saturday morning films – Flash Gordon at the local Bughouse, Sunday School, faggots for tea if we were lucky, got beaten by the teachers – great days. But Hold on – how did this turn into a nostalgia session for the good old days? Haven't we moved from the point?

Me: Well not really. In the last few years we've had to cope with increased terrorism, identity theft, cloning, big brother, massive immigration, international criminals, Murdoch, Fox News, Trump, Brexit, space shuttles, Higgs-Bosun

You: Higgs who? You're having me on!. How did he get into the picture? Sounds like a new kind of scout's knot.

Me:: OK if it isn't of interest – but a group of scientists in Geneva have just re-crested the particle that produced the first big bang 15 billion years ago.

You: And spent a lot of my money doing it – haven't they better things to do with their time?

Me: OK Forget the Higgs-Bosun – sometimes these things lead to new inventions that are part of everyday llfe. But perhaps I'm boring you – where were we?

You: Not me – you. You were spouting on about change – OK I get the point. Change is big, it's fast and getting faster. And it's a pain in the bum. I am getting bored, so get to the point!

Me: Yep – if you want to look at it that way. All I'm saying is that we can let these things happen to us poor sods on the bottom rung, or we can educate ourselves to know a bit more about what's happening – take an intelligent interest - so that, when we lose our jobs because of it, we know why. And can do something about it.

You: Like what?

Me: Well, develop our little grey cells, as that Belgian detective, forgotten his name,

You: You mean Poirot – and I sure wouldn't want to look like him! Looks like the rear end of an aardvark. What's all this got to do about the book? The Conflent Tales weren't they called?

Me: You remember the story about my neighbour, the peach farmer Armand? Most luscious peaches in the world? Well, he's now out of work – the peach trees developed a blight last year and half of them were cut own. And he isn't the only one – another 30 out of the 60 peasant farmers in the valley have gone the same way.

You: OK – I remember that bit – that's sad but it happens. Not my business.

Me: Well, in a way it is. You're an electrician, right? Safe job?

You: You bet! Safest job in the world. There'll always be a need for electricians.

Me: You sure – that's what the cotton spinners thought. Latest developments in the industry suggest that there'll be a lot more do-it-yourself easy to apply led kits available in a few years.

You: I know that – I'm keeping myself up to date.

Me: Good for you – look now – you're lifelong learning. But doesn't that mean that we'll need fewer electricians?

You: Come to think of it you're right but not me!

Me: You know? That's exactly what Armand said. Now he's on the dole, He's a peasant – proud to be a peasant. Doesn't want to do anything else but peasant his way through life. Won't retrain – thinks he's incapable at 45. Like all his mates up the road.

You: Now I'm getting worried Wish I hadn't started this conversation. What's your point!

Me: I suppose that I'm trying to say that there are lots of reasons why we should continue to learn throughout our lifetime , for jobs, for understanding the world we live in, for preparing retirement. For preventing Alzheimers.

You: Alzheimers. Now you're going too far. Nothing we can do about that

Me: There's a lot of research that says lifelong learning prevents Alzheimers – basically it boils down to use it or lose it.

You: Well I did see something recently about the number of people on evening school courses going up. And there's that new programme on tv called the Learning Channel. But I wouldn't call that Lifelong Learning.

Me: Nor is it, but at least lots of people are tapping into their own genius. Believe me, this thing is big - it's going to influence everyone of us and our childrens' children over the next century. And we are just at the beginning of the process. It's an exciting time.

You: Hold on a minute. Are you telling me that something this big is happening all around me and I don't know a thing about it?

Me: That's about the story. But I reckon you do know. Ever heard of downsizing?

You: Yup, I think so. It means that big companies are shedding a lot of workers. Thank the Lord it hasn't happened to me yet.

Me: Got it! Company executives call it right-sizing just to kid you that it's not really about getting rid of staff - but the effect is the same. Some companies have lost more than a third of their staff - In a company of 30,000 workers that's 10,000 people. And it's continuing. Ever heard of a guy called Handy?

You: Nope. Does he run the Handyman shop round the corner?

Me: He might but it isn't the one I'm talking about. Anyway, Charles Handy's a management guru and he writes and thinks a lot about the future of work. One of the formulas he's dreamed up is half x 2 x 3.

You: That's a nice formula - the answer's 3. What's on the other side of the equation?

Me: A lot of grief, believe me. He's talked to a lot of industrialist iron-heads over the years and the message he gets is that they are aiming to employ half the staff, pay them twice as much and get at least 3 times the productivity out of them - hence the half x 2 x 3.

You: Double the pay huh? I'm all for that.

Me: And half the workers out of the window! It could include you.

You: Is that why there's so much unemployment?

Me: In a simplistic way yes it contributes - but there are other reasons to do with low inflation and automation - complicated things like that. Anyway, Here's the good news - those jobs haven't all gone away. Those companies hire in people on contract to do the jobs they no longer employ people full time to do.

You: That's great. So we all get to stay in work.

Me: Some of us do, because here's the bad news for some. These new people have to be highly trained and accountable - they'll come from small companies, often one-man bands and they have to keep themselves continuously updated with new techniques and tools to do the job. And so do those core people employed by the companies. Everything's changing constantly and there's no shelter from having to learn continuously.

You: So what does that mean?

Me: Well, for a start, we've moved into a new and different sort of employment situation. You and me, we came to expect to be employed in one job for a lifetime. That's no longer true for most of us and is becoming even less true for future generations. The workers of tomorrow - that's our grand-children - will have several different jobs, several different careers - they'll have to be adaptable and flexible and versatile, mentally as well as geographically - they'll constantly need to be trained and retrained to a much higher level than today, and they'll have to dip in and out of education to renew their store of knowledge, skills and understandings. That means being switched on to Learning and knowing how to learn.

You: So is that what you call Lifelong Learning?

Me; It's what some people call Lifelong Learning. Me, I'd just call it Continuous Personal Development, Ever read the report on skill shortages published by the European Commission?

You: You're joking aren't you.

Me: Perhaps, but it says that in every country of Europe, including the UK, the requirement for manual and semi-skilled workers will go down by 20 % and the need for highly qualified people will go up by about 15%. Same thing will happen whether Britain's there or not. That's not good news for the underqualified.

You: Ho hum? So what, they can always get qualified, can't they? I did.

Me: It also says that even those who stay in the same job will have to be continually updated and take in the new technologies that will be used to stay in the job. Sometimes, dear friend. the world is having more influence on you than you're having on the world.

You: OK. So we're going to be forever learning new things. Learning's in. Staying put's out. Point made. Thanks for the lecture. Can we go home now?

Me: Hold on! It also says that countries and companies which don't invest in making people employable and keeping them updated are letting themselves in for a lot of misery.

You: OK, OK, So we should be investing in education instead of taking the tax cuts. Is there any more? Now I know what Lifelong Learning is.

Me: Not really - I haven't got round to that yet. All we've talked about is more about Continuing Education - keeping up to date and responding to new needs - things like that.

You: Jeez! You mean there's more? My brain's starting to hurt. Can I have a rest? I never was much interested in education anyway.

Me: Rest whenever you like. If you like, stick a bookmark in here. When you're ready, try a few more words. But let's get one thing straight - this isn't boring old education we're talking about, it's about stimulating things like new lifestyles, new ways of thinking and bright new horizons.

You: OK. But don't confuse me with any more new information, I know what I think! Put another way, I've abandoned my search for truth and am now looking for a good fantasy.

Me: Now you're having *me* on. Is all this new to you?

You: Course it's new - but you pick some of it up from the telly. I suppose it's time I learned a bit more about it. I'll give you five more minutes. Is it new?

Me: No way. Plato was wittering on about something called 'Dia Viou Paedeia' 2000 years before Christ. He would because he was Greek. But for him it meant that every citizen had a duty to develop his or her own potential and participate in the activities of the city. Then, there was a Chinese philosopher called Kuan Tzu. In the 3rd century BC he said 'When planning for a year - sow corn, when planning for a decade - plant trees, when planning for a lifetime - train and educate men'. Sounds a bit sexist if you ask me, but I think that he meant humankind.

More recently, Arthur C Clarke, the famous Science Fiction writer, defined the minimum survival level of the human race as 'everyone being educated to the level of semi-literacy of the average university graduate by the year 2000.' Science Fiction writers are allowed to be apocalyptic. Remember HG Wells? War of the Worlds and all that? He said 'The whole of human history is a constant race between education and catastrophe' - he thought the latter was winning - and as we look around us at some of the more horrific and horrible activities of some of our fellow creatures, who can say he got it wrong.

You: Hey - that's a long speech and this is getting really heavy - but strangely I'm enjoying it. So what's different about this whatsitcalled - Lifelong Learning, today?

Me: You think this is heavy - you should try my other book on Lifelong Learning[1]. Personally, I don't think it's that heavy but it's a sight heavier than this. But in general, there's no

[1] Learning Cities, Learning Regions, Learning .Communities Taylor and Francis. ISBN 10 0 37175 9
Lifelong Learning in Action – Transforming 21st Century Education, Taylor and Francis ISBN 0 7494 4013 9

difference in the ideas. It's just the context that's making it into a must. One example. Let's imagine the earth is a large spaceship.

You: Which in one sense it is.

Me: Yup. All its life-sustaining functions depend on a delicate set of physical, biological and chemical relationships between each other and all the lives of the species they sustain.

You: Eco-systems, right? I'm not right behind the wall.

Me: Right on. Like I said, you're a genius, and so are we all. One of these species is more intelligent and therefore more dominant than any of the others. It has the power of reason, the ability to introspect, invent and produce ideas, and the ability to communicate easily.

You: That's us OK?

Me: That's us. For a long period of time this species lives in harmony with its fellow travellers in space. But then it finds a use for some of the materials the spaceship is made out of, and converts them into energy so that it can live a little more comfortably.

You: Coal? Oil? Gas?. What a price they are nowadays.

Me: This causes no problem until, within a very short period of time, the numbers of the species increase rapidly. So, not only does it start to burn up these resources like they were going out of fashion, but also, by doing this, it actually sows the seeds of its own destruction in the longer term by creating a hole in one of the spaceship's protective shields against harmful rays.

As if that weren't enough, it actually starts to kill off the other species to give itself room to live. It fouls its own nest by unbalancing the ecosystems which sustain the spaceship.

You: Listen I know all this stuff. I simply haven't had the time to do anything about it yet.

Me: OK so now this species creates a magic machine which multiplies its creative genius a million-fold, but only a small proportion of this dominant species knows how to use it properly.

You: That wouldn't be the computer by any chance, would it?

Me: Who's telling whom here? Anyway, most of them could have access and use this magic machine which would make them vastly more intelligent, more reasonable, more able to develop their own potential. But they don't

You: Why not?

Me: You tell me. Either they don't want to or they don't believe it's important or they 're lazy, or they've been switched off. Or whatever.

You: Switched off?

Me: George Bush Snr called it the Vision thing – something he didn't have much time for. St Exupery said - if you want to have a good ship built don't talk about collecting wood, and sawing planks and planning work - Talk about the endless ocean and the wild sea and the joy of discovering new lands. Something like that.

You: Strong stuff

Me: Isn't that life and death? And with an expected 3 billion new members of the human race in the next 50 years, learning to adapt has got to play a large part in the future for all of us.

You: OK, so that's why we need that sustainable development stuff?

Me: Yup! Either that or we believe that 5 billion lemmings can't be wrong.

You: OK, so I'm a lemming or a learner. That's clear if true. So what do I need to understand from that?

Me: Somebody, I forget who, said that some changes are so fast you don't notice them, others are so fast they don't notice you. Maybe they're just two of a hundred reasons why the 21st Century has to be the 'Learning Century' - because, unless it becomes just that, the alternative is more and more unhappiness, social disorder, deprivation, poverty and a breakdown of civilised and democratic structures. It's already starting with Trump and Brexit.

You: This is beginning to get depressing. I'd close the book if I didn't find it so fascinating - but cut out some of the big words OK?

Me: OK, but it'll be difficult.

You: So what can you and I do about it? Education isn't the most popular word in many peoples' vocabularies.

Me: That's true and that's why its image has to change. Maybe we should be finding ways to stop people switching themselves off. Maybe the age of Education is dead and we're going into a whole new era of Learning.

You: That's pretty drastic and I'm not buying it? Sounds like a revolution and nobody wants that.

Me: Well you could always refuse to adjust your mind and believe that there's a fault in reality.

You: What a patronising comment. OK - truce. Suppose I just forget that I'm an old reactionary for a while and go along with your fantasy. What does this new age of Learning entail?

Me: Well, I suppose that it means putting the learner in charge of the learning, whoever they are, wherever they are, whenever they want their learning, and however they want to receive it. No more force feeding information to be regurgitated back on paper in a set time. Giving people, and that includes kids, the skills that they need to move into a learning lifestyle – communicating, making decisions, solving problems, working in teams, self-management. Learning has to be fun – engaged in voluntarily just as it did when we were very young children. Making learning the engine of self-development. Bringing.....

You: hold on, hold on. Big words, big ideas, big speech big words, small brain. You're sounding like a bloody professor. Head in the clouds, Long on ideas, short on practical solutions. Treating us poor erks as if we're thick as turnips. Yeah. Sure I can work out what you're babbling on about but that's not how it is. It isn't real.

Me: Ooops sorry – Yes I do get carried away. As it happens I am a professor but I hope not one living in an ivory tower. You want reality? The reality is Armand – jobless and staying that way. It's the millions of other jobless in Europe because they have been let down by the system. It's the politicians who are out of their depth. If learning has to change, then every part of the system needs to take action - not just the education systems in the schools, colleges and universities, but the social, political, economic and cultural systems we've built up in our societies as well. It isn't just about education.. Learning has to become fun, enjoyable, a pleasurable thing to do - whether it is for work, for leisure or for life it has to become a part of our lives in much the same way as shopping or banking or playing games.

You: Long speech. My eyes are starting to glaze over. School? Learning? Fun? Can't see the connection myself. How can schools and colleges make it so?.

Me: For a start, begin to understand the needs of people, and that includes children, as learners - find out why, when, what and how people prefer to learn, discover new stimulating learning methods, spot the basic skills which people need in order to learn better - learning to learn, developing our potential, handling information, developing thinking skills - individually, in groups and in families - using computers and satellites and tv channels to provide new learning for renewed people wherever they want to receive it. Making people adaptable and flexible and versatile as they'll have to be when they live with uncertainty.

You: That's quite a list. Big words again. Are they really ready for this?

Me: Well, there are a few places where things are happening - one or two schools are creating programmes for continuously developing the skills of their teachers so that they can respond better to their own learning needs and those of children. Some universities are widening their intakes, taking in more mature students and modifying their courses and entry requirements so that they can be much more accessible to the world of industry and the community around. Those that do often get the treatment from the backwoodsmen that they're letting standards slip, but I see it as responding sensibly to the new world.

You: Be careful. I might be a backwoodsman myself. Is that all that's happening?

Me: Well no - as a matter of fact, the greatest breakthroughs have come in the workplaces. Modern companies reckon that their strength and their future lies in the performance of their people and that developing individual skills and values is the most important thing they can do if they want to survive in a very competitive world. So they use new technologies for cost-effectiveness and make the learning process more democratic. They call themselves Learning Organisations and reckon that this is at least as important as their performance as business or manufacturing organisations. Marks and Spencer is a good example - it is becoming a true Learning Organisation.

You: What dear old Marks and Spencer a Learning Organisation? Why, it nearly went bust a few years ago.

Me: Dear old Marks, indeed - it's one of the country's most efficient companies now. It has to be because every other retailer is also a Learning Organisation. All their workforces have a big say in what happens and how things are done. That's why they need to learn, and learn fast. Ever heard of empowerment?

You: Well, well. Would you believe it? Marks and Spencer. So what's empowerment?

Me: It's what Marks and a lot more companies have given to their workforces. It means that the decisions are made down the line, where the work is, by the people who do the work. No more levels of hierarchy telling people what to do and how to do it. Hierarchies are flat. The employees themselves have to learn to make intelligent choices based upon what the outside marketplace needs. In other words, they're empowered.

You: Sounds like a recipe for disaster to me. But could that be because I'm behind the times?

Me: Could be. But it sure makes people responsible for their own company and they work and think a lot harder because they know that the decisions they make will, or won't, keep them in a job.

You: I can understand that. I'm much more motivated if I own the work I do. But doesn't it mean that they've got to have some pretty high-level skills and where do they get those from?

Me: You're learning. And it isn't all gravy. The companies themselves spend a lot of money putting their employees into the habit of learning. In an ideal world the schools, colleges and universities would be turning out adaptable, flexible and versatile people with high level analytical and teamwork skills but they've got a long way to go before that happens. Most of them are providing an education that was suitable in an industrial age for an environment that's now post-industrial.

You: Big word!

Me: Yes but you know what it means. The emphasis is still on information and remembering rather than knowledge, high-order skills, understanding and values - teaching what to think and commit to memory, rather than how to think and how to discriminate between good, bad and indifferent. In an age in which the amount of information available doubles every 5 years and then feeds upon itself to produce new knowledge, this is a nonsense.

You: This is all getting very abstruse. Isn't it the Government which tells education organisations, particularly the schools, what to do?

Me: Unfortunately yes. We can, and do, all have a go at Governments. They have financial levers and use them to get their own way. That's why there is a need for a change of mind-set, if the first part of the word can be located, in all parts of the system. Government has an important part to play in understanding and creating the conditions for the sort of Lifelong Learning Society that lets both nations and the people prosper economically and mentally.

You: What sort of a part would that be?

Me: It's firstly all about money. Here's a cliché. The economic health of a nation depends on the learning health of its citizens.

You: We've been through that and I buy some of it. Have governments bought it too?

Me: Some have, some haven't. Some have bought it and still work from dogma and prejudice. It's what buys the votes.

You: You cynic you! So what should they work from?

Me: Well, proper research for a start would help so that we can all understand what needs to be done. Then, a concentrated promotional campaign to let everyone know the what, the why and the how. Take all this talk about standards, for example.

You: OK. What about standards? We've got to keep up standards.

Me: Sure we have, and we have to have some measurement system to assess them. But do we need to have an examination system with built-in failure - that is one which creates failure in some in order to celebrate success in others?

You: Sure - that's the system. If you don't meet the requirements you don't deserve to pass.

Me: Well there are other, less divisive models - suppose for example we say that the objective of the whole thing is to develop the potential of each human being. Then we might want to use examinations mostly as a part of learning itself and to give the sort of feedback which guides the learner to eventual success. Let's call it a target-based system. If the learner isn't there yet, the results should say so and recommend what needs to be done to get him or her to the learning goal. No value judgements, no failure, no league tables, just encouragement. Sure, successful learning must be celebrated and rewarded, but let's make it possible for everybody, or as many as possible, to participate in the fun of success.

You: Hm! I'm not sure about that. Give me time to think about it. Mind-set change takes time. But there's something missing here. Why should people put themselves out? Isn't it a question of changing attitudes?

Me: Great question. You're switching on. Of course Lifelong Learning values and attitudes are as important as Lifelong Learning skills and knowledge. Ask anyone over 30 what they remember about their schooldays. Very few will mention subjects and classrooms. Most will remember the extra-curricular events, the games, the plays, the choirs, the camping holidays, the playground activities where values and attitudes were created – perhaps even the bullying. That's where I developed my love of music, I hope some consideration for others, and a talent for acting. I got them from participating in plays and choirs rather than being told about them.

You: Me too. Most things I like best because I like doing them.

Me: But don't values go further than people? In my ideal world, organisations have values - a company develops a set of values about the worth of its people and invests in their development accordingly. Schools, colleges or universities develop a set of values which let their students flourish. They are all investing in a lifelong learning future for their people and their economic future. Like we said, a well-governed nation promotes certain values as an investment in social cohesion and economic progress. That's an exercise in survival in a competitive world as well. A Learning Region whether it is a city, a town or a region tries to instil into its citizens the values of co-operation and harmonious living.

You. Oh boy – more headache and just as I thought this lesson was coming to an end. Now you're ahead of me again when I thought I'd caught up. What's a Learning Region?

Me: OK you asked for it! Here's the spiel. But I sense that you want the answer in 4 words and that's too much of a challenge. So here's the shortest answer I can think of. It's a city, town or region, in which every part - business and industry, schools, colleges, universities, cultural organisations and local government - cooperates closely so that it can become a great place to live and learn. It's the future for any place that wants to prosper in a competitive world. It's a lot of other things as well but I'm not going to bore you with the details.

You: Well, that's a blessing. Big speech! Who's been spreading the fairy dust? What sort of a world do you inhabit? There's only one place you'll find that - in heaven. You're flying into the realms of fantasy. It won't ever happen!.

Me: Sure it's a dream - and it might be impossible. I don't know - and we'll never know if we don't try it. But it's a great deal better than what we have now, and what's wrong with ideals? We all need ideals to keep us using our mental juices and looking outwards at the world. Anyway, we're not starting from a blank page. Believe it or not, just like lifelong learning it's now Government and regional policy in thousands of cities, regions and countries. Technology's a wonderful thing and makes a lot of things possible - look at how we've developed since the first Sputnik only 30 odd years ago. And it sure beats war and confrontation.   .

You: OK, I accept all that, but I still think that you're still in the land of the magic mushrooms. Where's the practical bit? Where's the reality? Give me a for instance

Me: OK. For instance, in the late 1970s, I set up a scheme between Woodberry Down School in inner-city Hackney in London and IBM Basinghall Street in the City – and you can't get two organisations more different than those, believe me. We called it schools-industry twinning. In theory it meant that the skills, knowledge and talents of more than 500 highly qualified professionals were put to the service of the education of staff and children at the school. This was a two-way cooperation and so the educational skills and knowledge and the facilities of the school were made available to the company. We had 30 projects and everybody benefited - teachers, children, employees, managers. Stereotypes broke down and both organisations learned a lot from the interaction between two dissimilar organisations. Energy flowed creatively.

You: So what sort of things happened then? And why doesn't it work now?

Me: Well, teams of people came to help school-leavers with interviewing skills and set up mock interviews for the kids to let them know how to get a job. Teachers came on management courses with people from industry and learned a lot of new skills. Kids spent a day looking at how people worked and what they did. Paper, equipment was made available for teaching purposes. The kids made an enormous collage for the boardroom.

You: Sounds good. There's probably a lot a school could do if it only found out and used what's available to it in the community.

Me: You bet! For example, there are at least 50 retired Brits here in the Conflent with teaching qualifications and enormous experience world-wide who would be willing to assist occasionally in the local school without payment. Maybe once a week, a month. They could add immeasurably to the kids' performance and learning enjoyment in languages and other subjects.

You: So why don't you offer?

Me: I did. I talked to the language teacher and several others.

You: And.......

Me: They didn't bite. They were affronted. They thought it was a threat to their authority rather than an opportunity to enrich the kid's education. That happens in most schools and it shows just how far we have to go. And it's not just schools. Think how much a University could contribute to regional development – all that knowledge and all that energy. Only happens in a few places there too.

You: So we've finally got to the bottom line and we can all go home. Lifelong Learning is about developing these things called Learning Regions to put this right?

Me: Sorry - not just that - that's a means to an end. Lifelong Learning is principally about people - you, me, the others - and how we can develop our own enormous human potential. In some cases, people have been so scarred by their learning experiences that they have been put off it for life. You might be one of them.

But that doesn't mean that the potential isn't there. Wasn't it Einstein who suggested that none of us, not even himself, ever use more than one-third of the capacity of our brains? We're all capable of learning and we're all capable of enjoying learning. But many people put limitations on themselves. Good Lifelong Learning practice takes away those limitations and provides us all with new tools, new horizons s and new motivations to learn. A yearning for learning.

You: OK, I'll buy it, with reservations. I'm thinking of returning to learning. So what has all this got to do with the Conflent?

Me: These are not just home thoughts from abroad - they're more abroad thoughts from home. You see, although Maggie and I have retired to this Paradise it doesn't mean that we have given up on the rest of the world. We're still turning to learning. That the world has problems is not in doubt - even this paradise has problems. For example, one can foresee a time when fruit-growing is no longer a viable occupation in this valley. Farmers here are not doing as well as they used to. Time, competition, disease, changes in the weather are already taking their toll. Two years ago the problem was blamed on hailstorm in the spring, last year it was the late frost - this year it is blamed on the *mévente*, people not buying, and Brussels allowing the import of cheaper Italian and Greek peaches. Local farmers tipped lorryloads of peaches onto the roads to bring attention to the problem.

You: They didn't!.

Me They certainly did. We got caught up in it twice. Farmers get 1.5 francs per kilo for dumping them officially and it costs them 4.5 francs per kilo to grow them. Most of them barely break even. In reality there is probably an overproduction and a self-pricing out of the marketplace partly because of the differential in incomes with other countries.. Some of this can be improved by a better distribution system. I told you about the high quality of the peaches.

You: Do I remember? Something about melting in the mouth. I was quite envious.

Me: OK, the problem's one of distribution. The peaches you eat in England and elsewhere are picked some weeks before they are ripe because of the delays in the transportation system. That's why they tend to be smaller and not so juicy. Some of us *britanniques* talk about making our fortunes by hiring a refrigerated lorry to take them to England twice a week. It's all talk of course - we wouldn't know how to begin. But even with this the fundamental problems won't disappear. Peach trees have a disease which will overtake them in time. Just as the coal-mines in the UK and the steel plants in Germany and the silk industry in Lyon and the linen industry in Ireland have simply disappeared, throwing thousands of people out of work, so peach farming in the Conflent will disappear quite quickly. And the Conflent is already an area of high unemployment.

You: So what is anybody doing about it? And what are the alternatives?

Me: Not a lot at present I don't think. We're not a Learning Region. Good planning has to be done years ahead - its not just here but everywhere that that's true. Even this corner of paradise is not immune from the great changes which are overtaking Europe and the rest of the world. The base economy of the region will diminish in value and some, only a few, local minds are beginning to think about the alternatives. One of these is tourism and if this book has helped to attract more visitors to the Conflent, then we shall have done our bit to stimulate the local economy. But if the Region wants to survive as a fruit-growing area then it will have to think of some alternative things to with the fruit – canning, liqueurs, bottling, fruit juices and so on.

Not of course that the farmers would quite see it that way. We are forever discussing alternative crops and land uses with our neighbours, who are among the more open-minded of the *agriculteurs* and always we end the discussion with no plan of action - the thought of turning the local fields into a huge golf course with my *mas* overlooking the 18th green appeals to me, but not, unsurprisingly, to my neighbour, who thinks little of golf and knows even less.

You: I can't blame him. Golf isn't my cup of tea either.

Me: Quite. But it's only an example. There's one in the golfer's tale. Some Scottish investors wanted to build a golf course up in Marcevol some 10 miles away. The money wouldn't even have to be provided by the region. But it fell foul of the professional protesters, the farmers, the planning authorities, the ecologists who wanted nothing to change. It could have started the creation of the region as a golfing paradise and brought much-needed employment. It isn't the only example where inward investment has been rejected by change-deniers here.

You: Yes, well. We get that in Britain too, look at the furore over wind farms. Not in my Backyard.

Me: Quite so. And yet, being ready for change can turn problems into challenges. Being willing to change can turn challenges into opportunities. Very few people like change, but it's built into all systems and societies now, and none of us can stop the world and get off. So we have to transform the mindset and look at uncertainty as a chance to do something different, rather than wait for poverty to arrive. Easily said, less easily done.

You: Too true. And I suppose that learning people in a proper Learning Region would support each other to make the best things happen.

Me: Now you're thinking creatively. It's a place where people learn easily and well, are adaptable to new ideas, look out to new opportunities and can turn their hands to a variety of things. Innovation and creativity, the fruits of learning, but I fear it won't happen with present mind-sets.

You: How about you. Where does this leave you in the Conflent?

Me: Maggie and I are learners and adapters. We have spent most of our adult lives in a variety of jobs, she as a casualty nurse, a district midwife, a doctors receptionist, a general nurse, a neuro sister and finally a researcher into the control of pain. She has had to constantly learn and relearn in order to stay up to date and progress in her various fields. Me, I have worked as a schoolteacher, as an education developer, salesman and systems analyst in industry. I've run European professional associations and worked internationally as a university professor - again a lifetime of learning. And we have moved around quite a lot – London, Paris, Brussels etc.

We didn't come to the Conflent to retire from learning - in fact when I have retired from my globetrotting activities, I intend to catch up on all the things an active life and an employer who bought my soul (no - it wasn't Mephistopheles it was IBM) prevented me from doing - to read for example Flaubert, Beaumarchais and Proust (for my sins), to travel for pleasure and enjoy the places I never saw on business, to go back to learning German, to start an English literary society, to put something more into the community, to become a gardener, building expert and carpenter, to keep fit enough to play tennis when I am 90 and golf when I am 100, to speak French more fluently, to play the piano a lot less badly than I now do, to publish my Ramsbottom poems and to write a novel, a play and a musical. And that's just the real list - the fantasy list is longer.

There is a delicious thought in one of Terry Pratchett's novels (now there's a man with more original ideas on one page than in the whole of this book) of scientific discoveries being floating particles of matter which settle at random on any living creature. Thus they are the product of chance - the first fish to step out of the water is a case in point - many other creatures had had the idea attached to them previously but this was the first one capable of saying to itself - I can breathe this stuff. Throughout the centuries there have been primitive earthworms, wise old owls, sweet daffodils all bursting to reveal the truth about the theory of gravity until the particle containing that knowledge settled on a brighter apple than most and dropped on a human head. And don't get the idea that Archimedes thought of the theory of the displacement of water, - he only communicated it - it was a tiny organism in his sponge which transferred the thought. For all I know the nightingales in our wood are singing $e=mc^2$, totally oblivious that someone already got there first. And as for the secret of time travel, well who knows what secret knowledge is contained in the brain of some three-toed sloth in the Brazilian jungle. And no, of course I don't believe that, but the creative power in people like Terry Practchett is what will sustain the world in the future.

That aside, developing our potential is really life's last challenge and the Third Age is a great time to do it. With advances in medical technology, many of us can expect to live into three figures, but what is that worth if the mind doesn't accompany the body beyond 80? Even if we live to be two hundred, we will never saturate the potential that is between our ears.

Many of us wish we had started earlier. Earning money has enabled us to live - the act of learning adds meaning to life, makes it worth while and fulfils our humanity. If Ministries of Education were called Ministries for the development of human potential, schools were organisations for the opening up of minds, universities institutions for the further development of human potential and industry organisations for the practical application of human intelligence, perhaps they would go about things in a different way and our whole lives would be different.

Focusing on developing learning human beings is the only way we can cope with the changes we're all going to have to face. To quote some guy called anon -'people are candles to be lit not vessels to be filled.'

You: Hey, that's quite an inspiring speech – at least the bits I could understand. Suppose, and it's only suppose mind, I wanted to find out more about this Lifelong Learning Region stuff. What do I do.?

Me: Well, being very modest of course, you could do worse than go to Amazon and order the books I mentioned earlier. It tells you what we might all expect from a Learning Century. More than that it contains some suggestions which everyone can take up to do something about it. Go to it! And Vive le Learning Conflent.

And apologies for inflicting such a serious topic ion such a light-hearted book. But isn't it just the point of the book in the first place?

So let me just finish with a last poem , written of course by me. It's a homage to the magic mountain that stands at the heart of this wonderful countryside, the Canigou.

A Canigou walk

I walked up the Canigou last Saturday
Not for the first time I venture to say
Each time it gets harder to complete the way
Up to the top

I drive to the refuge in a rusty old jeep
It means I can get just a little more sleep
It's enough to make a true mountaineer weep
To get to the top

The Canigou Assault Party sets out from base camp –
who will perish in the attempt?

I have to confess it's a bit of a slog
I'd probably do better with a guide dog
Fit folk would run at a moderate jog
Up to the top

My grandson, aged seven, soon set to the chase
My son in his forties walked at a fast pace
 I crawled like a snail halfway from the first base
Up to the top

But when I get there the rewards are intense
Time to let self-adulation commence
The views from the summit are truly immense
Up at the top

I think that's the last time I'll observe this chore
My muscles and joints just won't take any more
I'll just find a lift in a secret back door
To get to the top

Bye.